The Big Ideas Club Presents
Poetic Philosophy
Narrative Translations Designed for Accessibility

Philo of Alexandria's:
On the Creation Given by Moses

A Jewish Philosophy of Cosmic Reasoning

By Philo of Alexandria

Translated by Jason Kassel, PhD
© 2025
Recursive Publishing

Part I: Moses the Law-Giver: Beyond Plato's Completed Not-Corporeal Cosmos

I. Moses the Lawgiver (Theaetetus' Wax)

In a manner Bare and UnAdorned, offering only Commands without Beauty or Reflection, one type of Lawgiver handed down what they considered Just. Another type, by inflating their Doctrines with overwrought Ornament, mesmerized the Crowds and concealed Truth beneath Mythic-Inventions. But Moses, the Lawgiver, surpassed both kinds - rejecting the former as Crude, Toilsome, and Un-Philosophical, and the latter as Contrived and full of Enchanting Deceit. Instead, he fashioned the Beginning of his Laws as Supremely-Noble and Most-Reverent. He did not immediately declare "Do this" or forbid the opposite, nor - though it was necessary to shape the Minds of those who would follow the Laws - did he resort to Inventing Myths or borrowing Fictions composed by others.

Rather, as I said, Moses' Beginning is Most-Wondrous, for it contains a Creation of the Cosmos - a Beginning in which Law and Cosmos are brought into Harmony, each Mirroring the other. Thus, from the very outset, the Lawful Human becomes a Citizen-of-the-Cosmos, whose Actions are ordered in accord with the Will of Nature, by which the entire Cosmos itself is Governed.

The Beauty of the Ideas expressed in this Cosmos-Creation is such that no Poet, no Prose-Writer, could possibly Hymn it worthily - for it surpasses both Speech and Hearing, being of such Greatness and Reverence as to be unsuited to the Instruments of Mortal Beings. And yet, for that very reason, we must not remain Silent. For the sake of Love toward the Jewish-God, one must dare to speak beyond one's Power - not contributing anything of one's own, but offering a few Things in place of Many, as much as the Human Mind can reach when seized by Longing and Desire for Wisdom.

Just as even the Smallest Seal can receive the Imprint of Colossal Shapes, so too the surpassing Beauties of the Cosmos-Creation, as recorded in the Laws of the Jews, casting shimmering Shadows across the Souls of those who encounter them, may be outlined in brief - once we have first disclosed a Truth that must not be left unspoken.

II. Two Principles of Being (Timaeus)

There are some who, having marveled more at the Cosmos than at its Maker, proclaimed the World to be Not-Generated and Eternal. In doing so, they consigned the Jewish-God to complete Not-Activity - a stance both Not-Reverent and Unknowing. But the Truth demands the opposite: one must shape an account of the Divine-Powers in the image of an Artisan and Father - not glorify the Cosmos beyond its just Measure.

Now Moses the Lawgiver, having ascended to the very Summit of Philosophy, and having been thoroughly instructed in the most cohesive and binding Truths of Nature - through Structured-Revelations (χρησμοῖς), not through mere ecstatic utterances - clearly grasped that Being rests upon Two Principles: the one an Active Cause, the other a Passive Receptacle.

The Active Cause of Being, which governs all things, is Mind - the most Pure and Not-Mixed, more exalted than Virtue, more perfect than Knowledge, and superior even to the Good-Itself and the Beautiful-Itself.

By contrast, the Passive Cause of Being - moistureless, motionless in itself - is only stirred, shaped, and Ensouled through the Action of Mind, and is thereby transformed into the most Perfect of all Works: namely, this Cosmos.

Those who assert that the Cosmos is Not-Generated overlook the most essential and beneficial Doctrine for Piety: namely, Divine Providence - the very heart of Reverence toward the Jewish-God. For Reason dictates that the Father and Maker must care for what He has brought into Being. A Father tends His offspring; a Craftsman oversees what He has crafted. He removes all that is harmful or destructive with every kind of Skill, and He provides everything useful and beneficial in all possible ways.

But with what has not been made, there can be no relation for the One who has not made it. Such a view - denying Creation - is not only impossible to argue, but useless. It installs Anarchy within the Cosmos, just as in a City without Governance. It leaves the World without a Steward, a Judge, or a Ruler, under whose Authority all things might be Rightly-Administered.

But the great Moses, holding that the Not-Created is utterly Foreign to anything Visible, rightly assigned Eternity only to that which is Not-Visible and Intelligible - for all that is Grasped by the Senses is always in a state of Coming-to-Be and Alteration, and never fixed in True-Being. And so, he attributed Immortality to that which is Not-Seen and Intelligible, as to a Brother and Kindred of the Jewish-God, but gave to the Visible and Sense-Perceptible its proper name: Generation.

Thus, since this Cosmos is both Visible and Perceptible, it must necessarily also be Generated. Therefore, Moses did not record its Genesis without purpose, but in doing so, he performed an Act of most Reverent-Theology.

III. The Order Offered by the Number Six (Timaeus)

That Moses says the Cosmos was fashioned in Days is not because the Jewish-God, the Jewish-God, required a long span of time - for it is fitting that the Divine should Act all at once: not merely commanding, but also conceiving the Whole together. Rather, the Account unfolds in Days because what comes into Being requires Order. And Order is properly expressed through Number, and of all Numbers, that which - by the Laws of Nature - is most fertile and Generative is Six.

For Six is the first Perfect Number to arise from Unity: it is equal to the sum of its own parts and is completed by them - being one-half of the Triad, a third of the Dyad, and composed also of the Monad. So to speak, it is by Nature both Male and Female, joined together by the Powers of each. For in the realm of existing things: Oddness is Masculine, and Evenness is Feminine. Among Numbers, the beginning of the Odd is the Triad, the beginning of the Even is the Dyad, and their union produces the Hexad (Six), which combines the force of both.

Since the Cosmos is the most Complete of all things that have come into Being, it was necessary that its Completion take the form of the Perfect Number - Six. Moreover, since it was destined to generate future Becomings through Combination, it was rightly stamped with the first Even-Odd Number, which encloses within it the form of the Male who sows and the form of the Female who receives Seed.

Each of the Six Days was thus assigned one part of the Whole, and the Day that Moses withheld from the sequence - which he does not call the First, so that it would not be counted along with the others - he instead names "One," a term of directness and clarity, recognizing and proclaiming within it the Nature and Calling of the Monad.

IV. Archetypal and Intelligible Form (Timaeus)

We must now speak of whatever Elements can be expressed among those included in the Account, though in Truth the subject is beyond all Capacity - for the Creation Narrative encloses within it the entire Intelligible Cosmos, distinct and set apart, just as the Structured-Narrative concerning it suggests.

For the Jewish-God, precisely because He is He, understood, in advance, that a Beautiful-Imitation could never come to be without a Beautiful-Exemplar, and that no Apprehendable thing could be Blameless unless it were modeled upon an Archetypal and Intelligible Form. Wishing, therefore, to create this Visible Cosmos, the Jewish-God first sketched the Intelligible one, so that by employing a Paradigm that is Incorporeal and most Divine in its Nature, He might then fabricate the Bodily Cosmos - a younger Image of the elder, containing as many Visible Kinds as are contained as Intelligible Kinds in the Archetype.

Now, to speak or even to suppose that the Cosmos composed of Ideas exists in a Spatial Location is forbidden. But we may come to understand how it exists if we follow an Image drawn from our own experience. When a City is about to be founded, driven by the ambition of a King or Ruler - especially one who wields Sovereign-Power and wishes to Adorn his Good Fortune with splendid Achievement - there may come along a man educated in the arts: a True-Architect. Having observed the temperate climate and suitability of the site, he first traces within himself nearly all the parts of the City-to-Be: temples, gymnasia, council-houses, marketplaces, harbors, shipyards, streets, walls, foundations of private dwellings, and other public buildings.

And just as if he were imprinting Wax, he receives upon his own Life-Principle the Forms of each thing - and carries within himself a Statue-Bearing, Intelligible City. Then, stirring these Images with his native Memory and impressing the Archetypes even more deeply into himself, he, like a good Craftsman, looks always toward the Pattern and begins to construct the City from wood and stone, reproducing each of the Incorporeal Ideas in their Corporeal Form.

Thus, we must think similarly concerning the Jewish-God. Desiring to found the Great City, He first conceived its Archetypal Forms - and, assembling from them the Intelligible Cosmos, He then brought the Visible Cosmos to Completion, always using that Archetype as His model.

V. The Father and Craftsman is Good (Timaeus)

Just as the City first outlined by the Architect did not exist in any external space, but was impressed within the Life-Principle of the Artisan, in just the same way, the Cosmos composed of the Divine-Ideas could not possibly have any other place than within the Divine-Logos of the Jewish-God, who arranged and Adorned all these things. For what other Location could be sufficient to even receive and contain one of His powers - let alone All - especially if it were utterly unrestrained? Now, the Power of Creation itself - the one through which the Cosmos is made - has its source in that which is Truly and Absolutely Good.

If one were to inquire into the Reason why the Jewish-God made this All, I believe he would not miss the mark in declaring what one of the Ancients also rightly said: "The Father and Craftsman is Good." Because of His Perfect-Nature, the Jewish-God was not envious of Being itself, even though, before He Ordered, Being possessed the Not-Beautiful, yet had the Capacity to become All-Things. For in its prior condition, Being was full of Disorder, Shapelessness, Lifelessness, Dissimilarity, Otherness, Imbalance, and Disharmony. But it was capable of transformation - capable of receiving change toward the contrary and the better: toward Order, toward Form and Quality, toward Ensoulment, toward Likeness, toward Identity, toward Harmony and Proportion, and toward everything belonging to the Better Idea.

VI. In the Image of the Jewish-God (Timaeus)

There was no External-Counselor - who else could there have been? - and so the Jewish-God, using only Himself, determined that it was fitting to perform a Benefaction, freely and with lavish generosity, upon a Nature incapable of attaining any Good on its own without Divine-Gift. But He did not distribute His Benefactions in Proportion to their own magnitude - for these are Not-Bounded and Not-Finite - but in Proportion to the Capacities of those who were to receive the Benefit. For just as the Jewish-God is by Nature disposed to perform Good, so too is the Receiving not always disposed to receive Good in kind. Since the Powers of the Giver surpass all Bounds, and the Recipients are too weak to grasp their full Measure, He would have refrained altogether - unless He had measured out the Gift according to a just Proportion, Balancing and Harmonizing what He gave to each according to their Capacity to Receive.

Now, if one should choose to speak in clearer and more direct terms, one could say nothing other than this: that the Intelligible-Cosmos is nothing else but the Divine-Logos of the Jewish-God already engaged in the Act of Cosmos-Creation. For the Intelligible City is nothing other than the Rational-Plan of the Architect as He is inwardly envisioning the founding of that City. And this Doctrine is not mine - it is the Doctrine of Moses. For in describing the Generation of the Human-Being, Moses explicitly confesses that the Human was fashioned "in the Image of the Jewish-God" (Genesis 1:27).

If even the part is the Image of the Image, then clearly the Whole must be as well. And if this entire Sense-Perceptible Cosmos is greater than the Human-Being, and is likewise a Likeness of a Divine-Image, then it is evident that the Archetypal Seal - the one we call the Intelligible Cosmos - is none other than the Divine-Logos itself: the Paradigm, the Archetypal-Form of Forms.

VII. Time (Not-Timaeus)

Jewish-Scripture says, "In the Beginning, the Jewish-God made the Heaven and the Earth." By invoking this "Beginning," Moses is not referring - contrary to what some suppose - to a Temporal Beginning. For Time did not exist before the Cosmos. Rather, it came into Being either simultaneously with the Cosmos or afterwards. This is because Time is the Measured-Interval of the Cosmos' Motion, and no Motion can exist prior to the thing that is moved. Therefore, Time must either be of the Same-Age as the Cosmos or be Younger than it. To declare Time as Older is to speak with Not-Philosophical recklessness.

If then, "Beginning" does not mean the Beginning in Time, it must mean the Beginning in Number. So the phrase "In the Beginning, He made the Heaven" means: "First, He made the Heaven." And this is fitting - for Heaven is the most Excellent of all Things that have come into Being. It is formed from the most Pure portion of Substance, and is thus most rightly appointed as the Holy-House for Visible and Perceptible Gods.

Even if the Creator fashioned all Things at once, there would still be an Order in those Things that were well-fashioned. For there is no Beauty in Disorder, and Order consists in Sequence and Coherence - where some Things precede and others follow. This is true, even if not in their outcomes, then at least in the Mind of the Artisan while Crafting them. Only in this way could all things be made with Precision, without Confusion, and without Error.

So then, the Jewish-God first made: the Heaven, as Not-Body and Intelligible; and the Earth, as Not-Visible; and the Form of Air; and the Void. The Void He named "Darkness," for Air by nature is black; and the "Abyss," because the Void is bottomless and without limit.

Next, He made the Incorporeal Substance of Water, and of Breath, and above all these, a Seventh Light - which again was Incorporeal and Intelligible - a Paradigm of the Sun and of all the Light-Bearing Stars that would be set in the Heaven.

VIII. Breath and Light (Not-Timaeus)

Among all the things that came into Being, Breath and Light were granted Pre-Eminence. The Breath was named as belonging to the Jewish-God, because it is the most Life-Giving of all things - and the Jewish-God is the

Cause of Life. The Light was declared to be Exceedingly Beautiful (Genesis 1:4). For the Intelligible Light surpasses the Visible Light as much as - if one may speak by analogy - the Sun surpasses Darkness, Day surpasses Night, and Mind surpasses the bodily Eyes: for Mind is the Governor of the Whole Life-Principle.

Now, this Not-Visible and Intelligible-Light is itself the Image of the Divine-Logos - that same Divine-Logos who Interpreted and Brought-Forth its Generation. It is a Heaven-Beyond-Heaven Star, the Source and Fountain of all the Perceptible Stars. And one would not be wrong to name this source the All-Origin-Star (Panēgetēs) - from which the Sun, the Moon, and the other wandering and fixed stars all draw forth their radiance, each according to their own Capacity. These Stars receive their proper brightness from that Not-Mingled and Pure Light, which dims when it begins to descend and is transformed - from its Intelligible to its Apprehendable condition. For nothing that is grasped by the Senses remains Pure.

IX. Darkness (Not-Timaeus)

It is well said in Jewish-Scripture that "Darkness was upon the face of the Deep" (Genesis 1:2). For, in a certain way, Air surpasses the Void, having spread out and filled the entire vast, desolate, and empty region stretching from below the Moon down to us. But once the Intelligible Light - which existed before the Sun - had begun to shine forth, its Opponent, Darkness, began to recede. This separation was wrought by the Jewish-God, who set a dividing wall between the two and kept them apart, knowing well the opposition of Contraries and their natural tendency toward conflict.

So that these Opposing Powers might not forever clash and contend - so that War might not triumph over Peace, thereby imposing Disorder within the Cosmos - the Jewish-God not only separated Light from Darkness, but established Boundaries between them, fixed Intervals in the middle, which would contain each extreme. For being neighbors, the two were always at risk of Chaotic Intermingling, continually striving against one another in their unending Rivalry for Dominion. If not for the Middle-Intervals set between them, this collision would never have ceased.

These Middle Boundaries are called Evening and Morning. Morning foreshadows the rising of the Sun and gently repels the Darkness. Evening follows the setting of the Sun and calmly welcomes the return of Darkness. Yet we must understand both Morning and Evening as belonging to the realm of Incorporeal and Intelligible Things. There is nothing of Sense-Apprehension in them - they are entirely Forms, Measures, Types, and Seals of Generation, giving shape to Incorporeal Templates of what will later appear in Body.

Once the Light had come into Being, and Darkness had stepped back and withdrawn, and the Boundaries -

Evening and Morning - had been fixed within the Intervals, Time was thereby Immediately Established through the necessary Measure, which the Jewish-God called Day. But he did not call it the First Day, but rather One Day - because of the Singular and Unifying Nature of the Intelligible Cosmos, whose archetype is always One.

X. The Visible Cosmos (Not-Timaeus)

The Incorporeal Cosmos had already reached its Completion, being founded and established within the Divine-Logos. The Visible Cosmos was now being brought to perfection in accordance with that Archetype. And first among its parts - the one that is Best of All - the Jewish-God, the Craftsman, made the Heaven, which He rightly called the Firmament, precisely because it is Bodily. For Body, by its very Nature, is Firm - since it has threefold extension. Yet the concept of a firm and extended body differs from that of something wholly disjointed and scattered.

It was therefore appropriate to set the Visible and Body-Like in opposition to the Intelligible and Incorporeal, and to name this Visible part the Firmament. Immediately after, He referred to it as Heaven - with complete accuracy and propriety. Either because it is the Limit of All Things, or because it was the First of All Visible Things to Come Into Being. After its Generation, He also assigned to it the name Day, placing upon the Heaven the whole Measure and Interval of Daytime. This was done because of the dignity and worth the Heaven possesses among all things Visible, thus giving it the honor of Second Place - the day following the first (or rather, the "One") that belonged to the Intelligible Archetype.

Part II: Moses Beyond Plato: Explaining Creation

XI. Water

After this, since the Whole Water had been poured out across the entire Earth and had visited every part of it - like a sponge soaked with moisture - the result was marshland and deep mud, a mingling and interweaving of both elements, Water and Earth, blended like dough into a single, undifferentiated, and shapeless nature. The Jewish-God then gave a command: the Water - which was briny and destined to become barren for seed and fruit-bearing trees - was to be drawn away and flow together, collected from the rarified channels of the Earth. In turn, the Dry Land was to appear, with just enough sweet moisture left behind to allow for continuity and cohesion. For this sweet and Proportioned moisture acts like a binding-glue among the separated elements.

And in order that the Earth not become utterly desolate and infertile, and so that - like a Mother - she might nourish not only one kind of food but both kinds (that which is for plants and that which will become food for offspring), the Divine allowed her to remain potentially fruitful, holding within her the power to give Birth.

XII. Earth

Then, He began to Adorn the Earth. For He commanded it to sprout grass and to bring forth grain-bearing stalks, unleashing every kind of herb and rendering the plains rich with verdure - all things that would serve as nourishment for both animals and human beings. In addition, He caused the Forms of all Trees to arise. Nothing was overlooked - neither what belongs to the so-called wild, nor what belongs to the cultivated. The Earth was immediately filled with fruit-bearing trees at the very moment of their coming-into-being - according to an order opposite to what prevails now.

For in the present state of things, Generation occurs by parts and across diverse spans of time - not all at once and in a single moment. Who does not know that first there is sowing and planting, then the growth of what has been sown and planted? One part extends roots downward, as though laying foundations; the other part is lifted upward in height, forming stems and stalks.

Next come shoots and the sprouting of leaves, and finally the bearing of fruit. But even the fruit is not immediately complete. It undergoes many transformations - in size, in form, in color - passing through every stage before it reaches completion. In the beginning, the fruit is like a tiny secretion, hardly Visible, which could be called the first Apprehendable in the sequence of becoming.

But gradually, by the nourishment channeled through the tree, and by the temperate Breaths of the atmosphere - those that are cool and gentle - it is kindled and nurtured, and so it grows in mass and reaches perfection. With that increase in size, it also changes in quality, just as if it were being painted and Adorned by a skilled hand in the art of coloring.

XIII. First Generation of All-Things

At that First Generation of All-Things - just as I said before - the Jewish-God summoned forth from the Earth the whole Plant-Matter, already in its perfect state, bearing fruits not unfinished, but already in full maturity, prepared for immediate and unsurpassable use and enjoyment by the Living-Beings who were soon to be brought into Being. The Divine commands the Earth to Generate these things. And the Earth, as if long pregnant and laboring in birth, brings forth all the varieties both of seed-bearing plants and of fruit-bearing trees, as well as the countless Forms of their fruits. But these fruits were not only intended as nourishment for Living-Beings - they were also intended as preparations for future Generations, containing within themselves the Seed-Substances, in which lie hidden and Not-Visible the Structured-Narratives (Logoi) of all the kinds of plants, which would later become revealed and manifest through the revolutions of the seasons.

For the Jewish-God willed to lengthen Nature's course - in a way, granting the kinds of living things a share in immortality, bestowing upon them a kind of perpetuity. For this reason, He bound Beginning to End and hastened End back to Beginning - so that the Cycle might be continuous. From the plant, then, the Fruit comes forth - as if the End from a Beginning - and from the fruit, again containing the Seed, the plant is enclosed within - as if from an End, a new Beginning emerges.

XIV. Heavens

And so, on the Fourth Day, after the Earth had been established, the Jewish-God set about Adorning the Heavens with Heavenly-Forms - not because He ranked the Heavens lower than the Earth by placing them later in the sequence. For while Earth was given priority in time, it belonged to the lesser nature, whereas the greater and more Divine Nature of Heaven was worthy of a second, more exalted moment in the unfolding. Rather, this order reveals most clearly the Sovereign Power of the Beginning. For foreseeing, in advance, the kind of people who would come into being - mortals inclined to reason by appearance and plausibility, preferring conjecture over Truth, and trusting more in what is Visible than in the Divine - He delayed the creation of the Heavenly Lights. These mortals, admiring the cleverness of reasoning rather than the wisdom of God, would later gaze upon the revolutions of the sun and moon and imagine that the seasons - summer, winter, spring, and autumn - and the growth cycles of all Earth-born things depend on the motions of the celestial bodies.

To prevent such people - whether through shameless arrogance or through ignorance swollen beyond measure - from boldly attributing causality to these later-born things, the Jewish-God says, in effect: "Let them return in their understanding to the First Generation of All-Things, when before the sun and moon existed, the Earth brought forth every kind of plant and every kind of fruit. And seeing this through the eyes of their mind, let them come to hope that the Earth will again bear fruit at the command of the Father, whenever it pleases Him - without any need for the assistance of His Heavenly offspring, to whom He indeed gave power, but not autonomy."

For just as a Charioteer directs his reins, or a Pilot steers by means of the rudder - each one controlling all motion in accordance with Law and Justice, needing no helper - so too does the Jewish-God govern. All things are possible for He.

XV. Tetrad (Plato's Three Becomes Four)

This, then, is the true Cause why the Earth had already blossomed and borne greenery, prior to the Adornment of the Heaven. For Heaven was being Adorned anew with the Perfect Number, the number Four, which no one would err in calling the source and fountain of the Decad, the Complete-Whole of all numbers. For the Decad is the Actualized-Unity of Number, and the Tetrad (Four) appears to contain its Power. Indeed, if one adds together the natural numbers from One through Four in succession, they will produce Ten:

$$1 + 2 + 3 + 4 = 10.$$

This Ten marks the Turning-Point from the Infinite Succession of Numbers - around it they curve like a cosmic arc, bending forward and returning again in rhythmic cycles. Now, the Tetrad also contains within itself the Proportional-Relations that generate Musical Harmony: the ratio of the Fourth (4:3), the Fifth (3:2), the Octave (2:1), and the Double Octave (4:1). From these, the most Complete and Perfect Harmonic System is born. The Fourth (diatessaron) corresponds to epitritos - the ratio four to three (4:3). The Fifth (diapente) corresponds to hemiolios - the ratio three to two (3:2). The Octave (diapason) corresponds to double - the ratio two to one (2:1). And the Double Octave (dis diapason) corresponds to the fourfould - four to one (4:1). All these Proportional-Relations are encompassed by the Fourfold Number (Tetrad), which contains the Seed of Cosmic Harmony, both numerically and musically, as the foundation of the Living-Whole.

XVI. Solid-Body (A Child's Game)

Moreover, there exists another Capacity belonging to the Tetrad - one that is astonishing both in Speech and in Thought. For it was this number that first revealed the Nature of the Solid-Body. All the numbers prior to it belong to the domain of the Not-Bodied.

In Geometric-Terms, the Monad corresponds to the Point. The Dyad corresponds to the Line - since the Movement of the One produces Two, and the Movement of a Point produces a Line. A Line is a length without breadth. When breadth is added to this, we arrive at the Plane - this is the Triad. Then, when depth is added to the Plane, we have the emergence of the Tetrad, and thus the conception of the Solid-Body.

Therefore, this Number Four is of immense significance: it marks the first transition from the Non-Bodied and Intelligible Essence to our Apprehension of a Three-Dimensionally Extended-Body - that which is, by Nature, the First Truly Apprehendable-Thing.

And if anyone does not immediately grasp this, let them consider a child's game - familiar to all - where three nuts are arranged on a flat surface, and a fourth is placed atop them, forming a pyramid. The base triangle extends to the Triad, but the addition of the fourth generates not merely the Tetrad in number, but a pyramidal form - a Solid Body.

And in addition to this, one must not overlook the following marvel: the Number Four is the first square number - equal times equal - a true Measure of Justice and Equality. It is also the only number that is generated both by addition and by multiplication of the same constituents: By addition: Two plus Two, and by multiplication: Two times Two. This reveals a Harmonious and Beautiful Form of Symmetry - a property found in no other number. For instance, Six is made by adding two Threes, but when multiplied (three times three), it yields Nine - another, entirely different number.

The Tetrad possesses many other Capacities, which should be more precisely explained in a separate discourse focused exclusively on its Nature. But for now, it is sufficient to add this: The genesis of the whole Heaven and Cosmos began with the Tetrad. For the Four Elements - from which this All was Crafted - stream forth, as from a Source, from the Number Four. And beyond this, there are also Four Seasons of the Year, which are the Generating-Causes for the birth of animals and plants: Winter, Spring, Summer, Autumn. These Four divide the Year into a Natural Rhythm and echo the Tetradic-Structure of All-Generation.

XVII. Vision (Most-Excellent Sense-Apprehension)

Since the Natural-Order granted such Great-Privilege to the Tetrad, by necessity the Jewish-God Adorned the Heaven in accordance with it - furnishing it with the Most-Beautiful and Divine-Like Order of Stars.

For the Light-Bearing Stars were arranged in this way, because Light itself is the Most-Excellent among Beings, and it is the Instrument of the Most-Excellent of the Sense-Apprehensions: Vision.

Just as Mind is the Governing-Element in the Life-Principle, so the Eye is the Ruler among the Organs of the Body. The Mind Perceives the Intelligible; the Eye Perceives the Apprehendable. And just as Mind requires Knowledge in order to grasp Non-Bodied Beings, so too the Eye requires Light to apprehend Body-Things. Now Light is the Cause of many Goods for Humanity - but especially of the greatest Good: Philosophy.

For when Vision is elevated upward by Light and gazes upon the Nature and Movement of the Stars - those that are fixed and those that wander - it sees their Harmonious Circular Motions. Some follow the same path consistently; others follow opposite or differing courses with dual rotations. The choreographed dance of all these stars, governed by precise Musical-Laws, brings forth an unspeakable Delight and Joy for the Life-Principle. And, as it is fed by the succession of these Visible Sights - one arising from another - it becomes insatiable in its desire to Gaze upon the Heavens.

Then, as is its Nature, Vision begins to ask: What is the true Essence of these Visible things? Are they eternal and Not-Created, or did they have a Beginning? What is the Nature of their Movement? What are the Causes that Govern each one's Motion and Role?

And it is from this kind of questioning that the Whole-Way of Philosophy arises - from which no higher Good has ever entered into the life of Man.

XVIII. Apprehendable-Stars (The Sun)

Turning now to the Intelligible-Light spoken of earlier as belonging to the Non-Bodied Cosmos - the Jewish-God crafted the Apprehendable-Stars as Divine-Statues which are Most-Beautiful and Sacred in Form. He established them in the purest sanctuary of Bodily-Essence: the Heaven itself. They serve many purposes: first, to give Light; second, to provide Signs; third, to mark out Seasons and Times associated with the annual rhythms; and finally, to define Days, Months, and Years. Thus, they have become the Measures of Time and the very Generators of Number.

The particular Use and Benefit provided by each Apprehendable-Star is evident from Experience, but for a more precise grasp, it is not inappropriate to track the Truth by Reason as well. Now the Whole of Time has been divided into two parts: Day and Night. The Father assigned authority over the Day to the Sun, as to a Great King. Night, by contrast, he entrusted to the Moon and to the multitude of the other Stars. The Power and Dominion of the Sun is clearly manifest: Though the Sun is only one among many Apprehendable-Stars, he alone governs half the cycle of Time - the Day. The Moon and all the rest govern the other half - what is called Night.

When the Sun rises, not only do the Images (phantasiai) of the Many-Stars lose their brightness, but they become entirely Not-Visible, being outshone by his Radiance. But when he sets, they immediately begin to reappear together, revealing once again their distinctive qualities in unison.

XIX. Apprehendable-Stars (Stars)

The Stars, as He Himself declared, came into Being not only to pour forth Light upon the Earth, but also to signal what is to come, making manifest signs of what lies ahead. By their risings and settings, by their eclipses, their reappearings and concealings, and by other variations in their Motions, humans attempt to forecast events yet to occur: the coming abundance or failure of fruits, the births and deaths of Living-Beings, conditions of clear skies or overcast, stills or tempests of wind, floods or recessions of rivers, the quiet or surging of the sea, and the transitions of the yearly Seasons - whether Summer grows wintry, or Winter blazes like Summer, whether Spring imitates Autumn, or Autumn takes on the bloom of Spring. Some have even dared to anticipate earthquakes and tremors of the Earth by means of speculation upon the Heavenly Motions. And so, countless other Unseen Matters, many unfamiliar to mortals, may yet be announced or caused by the stars, rightly making it entirely truthful to say: "The stars have come into being for the sake of Signs."

But also, as written in the Laws of the Jews: "for the sake of Seasons" (Gen. 1:14) - and by Seasons, He understood the annual divisions of Time, not without reason. For what else could Proper-Time mean, if not Time as it becomes Perfected in its use? Now the Seasons complete all things: sowings, plantings of crops, births and growths of animals and plants alike.

The stars have also come into being as measures of Time: through the cycles of the Sun and Moon and the other Wandering-Stars, they produce Days and Months and Years. And immediately there was revealed the most beneficial of all things - the Nature of Number, which Time itself seems to have led forth. From one Day came the Unit, from two Days the Two, from three the Three, from a Month the Thirty, from a Year the number equal to twelve Months of Days, and from Infinite Time, the Infinite Number. So necessary and manifold are the benefits that come from the Nature and Motion of the Stars in the Heavens.

And how many more things might I say, even now, of those mysteries that are hidden from us - for not all is Knowable to the Mortal-Kind - but which nonetheless contribute to the Preservation of the Whole? These things operate in accordance with Statutes and Laws which the Jewish-God has appointed as unchanging throughout the All, and which are therefore brought to completion in every place and in every way.

Part III: Moses Beyond Plato: How the Jewish-God Populated the Earth

XX. Fifth Day (Water-Dwellers) and Swimming Birds

Once Earth and Heaven had been Adorned with their proper Cosmic-Orders - Earth in Triadic-Harmony, Heaven in Tetradic-Perfection, as has been said - the Divine-Craftsman undertook the shaping of the Mortal-Kinds of Living-Beings. He began on the Fifth Day with those who dwell in the waters. For He judged that nothing is so bound by Nature to Living-Beings as the Five-Fold Capacity - since what distinguishes the Living from the Not-Living is Sense-Apprehension. And this, in turn, is divided Five-Fold: into Sight, Hearing, Taste, Smell, and Touch.

To each Sense-Apprehension, the Jewish-God assigned not only a distinct Material-Organ but also its own Judging-Criterion, by which it renders discernment over what falls into its grasp: Sight Perceives Colors, Hearing Discerns Voices and Sounds, Taste Discerns Liquids and Juices, Smell Recognizes Vapors and Exhalations, Touch Apprehends Softness and Hardness, Heat and Cold, Smoothness and Roughness.

And so, He summoned into Being all the kinds of fish and great sea-creatures, commanding them to arise in their varieties according to Place, Magnitude, and Qualities. Some He distributed among distinct seas, others He allowed to be shared across many; yet not all kinds were fashioned in every region - never without reason. For certain creatures thrive in shallow, marshy waters, while others prefer harbors and inlets, incapable of climbing upon the land nor swimming far from shore. Still others dwell in the deep, open sea, steering away from the projecting headlands, islands, or rocky coasts. Some flourish in calm and serenity, others in tempest and turbulence. Those struck repeatedly by surging waves are strengthened by resistance, driven upward by force, and so become more vigorous and dense in their composition.

At once, He also fashioned the kinds of birds, as siblings to the water-creatures - for both are, in their way, Swimmers: the one through waters, the other through air. Nor did He leave out any variety of these Winged-Kinds, completing each with precision, ensuring none were imperfect or left unfinished.

XXI. Land-Creatures

Now that Water and Air had received their allotted share of Living-Kinds, as if by a fitting inheritance, the Divine-Craftsman once again summoned the Earth to Bring-Forth the remaining kinds of Living-Beings - what had been left aside after the Generation of plants: namely, the Land-Creatures.

And so it is written in the Laws of the Jews: "Let the Earth bring forth cattle, wild beasts, and creeping things, each according to its kind" (Gen. 1:24). Immediately, the Earth brought them forth - each differing in Form and Structure, in strength, and in their Inherent-Powers, some being harmful, others beneficial. And above all these, He formed the Human-Being - we shall soon declare how,. For now, it is worth emphasizing that this unfolding followed a Most-Beautiful chain of succession, by which the Generation of Living-Beings had been narrated.

To explain: the Soul-Quality (ψυχή) that is Most-Sluggish and Least-Defined by Shape or Rationality was assigned to the Fish-Kind, whereas the Most- Finely-Formed and Fully-Actualized Soul-Quality belonged to the Human-Kind. The Middle Soul-Quality, intermediate between the two extremes, was given to the Land-Creatures and Airborne-Creatures. This Middle Soul-Quality is more Perceptive than the Fish's, but less Luminous than the Human's.

Thus, the fish, who share more of Bodily than Soul-Like Substance - creatures in a way alive and not-alive, moving-yet-soulless - were the first to be generated. Into them, a fragment of the Soul-Likeness was dispersed - not for the sake of spiritual life, but merely to preserve bodily existence, just as, they say, salt is added to meat so that it may not quickly decay. After the fish came the birds and land-dwellers - creatures of sharper Sense-Apprehension, whose very bodily construction reveals clearer signs of Soul-Presence.

And above all, as was said, came the Human-Being, to whom was granted a distinctive Mind - a Soul-beyond-Soul, like the Pupil within the Eye. Indeed, those who inquire most precisely into the Natures of Things declare that this Soul-of-Soul is itself the Eye of the Soul - and is to the Soul what the Eye is to the Body.

XXII. Seed-Origin and Soul-Capacities

At that moment, then, when the Sea was being Formed, all things were likewise Coming-Together into Being - and as they Came-Into Being Together, an Order was necessarily being Inscribed through Structured-Narrative, because this mutual Inter-Generation was about to unfold. Now, in the case of things that are generated one by one, the Order is as follows: the Beginning is made from that which is lowest in worth, and the Completion reaches toward that which is highest and most excellent. What, then, does this mean? We must make it clear.

The Seed-Origin of Living-Beings serves as the beginning of Generation. This Seed-Origin - when first observed - appears like mere foam, the lowest and most Not-Formed material. But once it has been cast into the

Womb and becomes firmly fixed, it immediately receives Motion, and this Motion is what Nature begins to shape.

Now, Nature is superior to the Seed-Origin, because, in the realm of Generation, motion is superior to stillness. Nature acts like an Artisan, or more precisely, she acts as an Infallible-Art, crafting Living-Forms, distributing the Moist-Essence into the various parts and members of the Body, and assigning the Breath-Like Essence to the Soul-Capacities - namely, the Nutritive-Capacity and the Sense-Apprehension-Capacity. As for the Rational-Capacity (Logismos), it must be placed above all, for some claim it enters from outside, being divine and eternal in nature. And so, Nature began from the base and insignificant Seed-Origin, but concluded in the most honorable of beings - the formed creature, the Living-Being, and above all, the Human Being.

This same pattern holds true also for the Creation of the Whole. When the Jewish-God decided to Form Living-Beings, the first in the Order of Creation were somewhat lower in value - namely, the fish. The last were the most excellent - the humans. And all the others in between - the land-dwellers and the airborne - stood as intermediates, better than the earlier, yet inferior to the later.

XXIII. Human-Beings Created in the Image-Form of the Jewish-God

Now that all other things had already come into Being, as previously recounted, the Laws of the Jews declare that the Human-Being was Generated - in the Image-Form of the Jewish-God and according to His Likeness (Gen. 1:26). And this is spoken Most-Beautifully - for nothing Earth-Born more nearly resembles the Divine than the Human-Being.

Let no one, however, suppose that this Resemblance refers to the Form or Shape of the Body. For the Jewish-God is not anthropomorphic, nor is the Human-Body in any way truly God-Shaped. The term "Image-Form" (εἰκών) is properly spoken with reference to the Ruling-Part of the Life-Principle, namely, the Mind. For just as there is One Archetype, the Mind of the All, so also in each particular Human-Being there has been Impressed a copy of that Archetype - a kind of Divine presence that the person bears within, as one might carry a Sacred-Statue.

For the same Structured-Narrative that the Jewish-God holds over the Entirety of the Cosmos, so too, it seems, does the Human-Mind hold within each person. Not-Visible itself, it Sees all things; Not-Knowable in Substance, it nonetheless Apprehends the Natures of others, navigating all paths - whether cut by the Arts or surveyed by the Sciences - in the many-branching pursuit of Knowledge.

Like a traveler, it walks every great road, journeying across Earth and Sea, investigating the Nature of both. Then, lifting itself like a Bird, it rises into the Air, observes all its affections, and ascends still higher, toward the Aether, to trace the Circular-Routes of the Heavens - both those of the Wandering Stars and the Fixed - joining their Dances, which proceed according to the perfect laws of Harmonic Music. Driven by Desire-for-Wisdom as its guide, the Human-Mind, having passed beyond all Perceptible Being, seeks to touch the Intelligible Realm. And of all that it once saw here in the Apprehendable World, it now beholds There as Archetypes and Ideal-Forms, surpassing all in Beauty. Filled with a sober intoxication, it is possessed - as those inspired by the Corybantic Rites - overflowing with yearning and desire for something Greater. And being led upward toward the Highest Summit of the Intelligible Things, it seems ready to approach the Great Jewish-God Himself.

But as it longs to Behold Him, a torrent of pure and unmingled Light pours forth like a flood, dazzling the eye of the Mind, causing it to tremble and grow dim from the intensity of the Radiance. Because not every Image-Form is fully Resembling to its Archetypal Paradigm - and because many are unlike - the Laws of the Jews adds the phrase "according to Likeness" (καθ' ὁμοίωσιν), to make clear that the Human-Mind is not just a distant reflection, but one bearing a clear, well-struck Imprint, a True-Type of the Divine Model.

XXIV. Human-Beings ('Let Us Make')

One might quite reasonably raise a difficulty here: why is it that, when it comes to the creation of the Human-Being alone, the Laws of the Jews does not attribute this work to a single Creator, as it did for all the other things - but instead, introduces the Jewish-God the Father of All speaking as if to many: "Let Us make Humanity according to Our Image-Form and according to Likeness?" (Genesis 1:26)

Is there really any need - so one might ask - for the Supreme Power, to whom all things are obedient, to summon assistance from any other? For when He made the Heaven, the Earth, and the Sea, He did not call upon any collaborators. How, then, could He be unable to fashion the Human-Being - this short-lived and fleeting animal - on His own, without the contribution of others? To be sure, the most truthful Cause is that the Jewish-God alone is the Jewish-God. But we are not forbidden from offering a likely interpretation, one that is plausible and reasonable to the ear.

Here, then, is such an interpretation: Among the things that exist, some are devoid of both Virtue and Vice - as is the case with Plants and Not-Rational Animals. The former are without Life-Principle and Governed by a

Nature Not-Capable of Form-Apprehension. The latter, though ensouled, are severed from Mind and Rational-Speech. Since both Virtue and Vice properly inhabit Mind and Rationality, only those Beings in whom Mind dwells can be said to contain these moral qualities.

There are, indeed, some beings - like the Stars - who share only in Virtue, and are Not-Touched by all Evil. These are rightly called Living-Beings, even Rational Living-Beings, or more truthfully still, Minds themselves - entirely Good, entirely unified, and entirely untouched by corruption. Then there are the Mixed-Beings, such as the Human-Being, who is capable of both contraries: of Wisdom and Folly, Moderation and Indulgence, Courage and Cowardice, Justice and Injustice - in short, of both Good and Evil, Noble and Shameful, Virtue and Vice.

Therefore, for the Jewish-God as Father of All, it was fitting to create what is Good by Himself - since such things bear a kindred likeness to Him. As for indifferent things, these too were not alien to His working, for Vice has no hold upon them. But when it comes to Beings of a Mixed-Nature, such as the Human, they are partly akin to the Jewish-God, by the nobler portion within them, and partly alien, by the baser element that dwells alongside. And for this reason, only with respect to the creation of Humanity do the Laws of the Jews declare that the Jewish-God said, "Let Us make" - a phrase that suggests the inclusion of others as co-creators or collaborators.

Why? So that, whenever a Human-Being lives in accordance with blameless Counsel and Right Action, the inscription of authorship might read: Jewish-God, the Ruler of All. But whenever one lives in the opposite direction, that authorship may be ascribed to others among His subordinates. For it was necessary that the Father remain blameless of Evil in the eyes of His offspring. And Evil, in truth, is Vice, and all actions that arise from Vice. And again, Beautifully, having declared the creation of Humanity, the Laws of the Jews then distinguishes the kinds by saying that Male and Female were created - even before their Forms appeared in the Structured-Narrative. This is because the most immediate types of differentiation already exist within the Genus itself, and, for those able to see sharply, Shine-Forth like Images in a mirror.

XXV. Human-Beings Came Last (Theological-Aesthetic Cause)

One might well inquire into the Reason why the Human-Being is placed last in the account of the world's Genesis. For it is evident, as the Laws of the Jews declare, that the Jewish-God and Father crafted the Human-Being after all the rest of Creation had already been completed. Those who have delved more deeply into the Laws, seeking with utmost care to trace and unfold every point with precision, explain the ordering thus:

When the Jewish-God bestowed upon the Human-Being a share in His Own Kindred-Nature - the Faculty of Rationality, which is the Highest and Most-Excellent of all Divine-Gifts - He did not begrudge Humanity any of the other Blessings either. Rather, as to one Most-Beloved and Most-Akin to Himself among all the Living-Beings, He prepared all that the World contains in advance - so that when the Human-Being came into Existence, he might find nothing lacking for either Living or Living-Well. For the First-Kind of Life - that of 'mere subsistence' - He furnished through the abundance of provision: the endless bounty of things suited for use and enjoyment.

But He supported the Second-Kind of Life - the 'Noble-Life' - by placing in view the Theory (θεωρία) of the Heavenly-Things. And from this Divine-Spectacle, when the Mind was struck with awe and yearning, there arose Desire and Longing for the Science of these matters. Hence, did the entire race of Philosophy spring up, by which even though he is mortal, the Human-Being is Divinized.

So it is, too, among banquet-holders: they do not summon guests to dine until all the elements of feasting have been readied. Likewise, those who arrange athletic games or dramatic spectacles do not call the spectators until the competitors, the performers, and the wonders to be shown and heard have been prepared.

In the very same way, the Jewish-God, acting as both a Feast-Master and a Game-Setter, intended to summon the Human-Being to partake in both a Banquet and a Sacred-Spectacle. He first made ready all that belonged to each Domain - so that, upon entering into the World, the Human-Being would immediately find laid before him a Holy-Banquet and a Theater of Divine-Grandeur. The Banquet, as it were, was filled with every provision - whatever the Earth and Rivers and Seas and Air might bring forth for use and delight. And the Theater - this too was stocked with marvelous sights: entities whose substances astonish, whose qualities overwhelm with awe, and whose motions and dances produce a sublime wonder.

These Theater-Movements unfold in Harmonious-Sequences, aligned with Proportional-Numbers and Cosmic-Cycles, all ordered in a rhythm of Divine-Symphony. In these Orchestrated-Harmonies, one could hardly be mistaken to say that the Original, True, and Archetypal Music is found - that Music from which all others take their pattern. And it was from this Music, implanted as Images in the Life-Principle that Human Beings, in time, gave rise to an Art Most-Necessary and Most-Beneficial to Human-Life.

Part IV: Moses Beyond Plato: Placing Judgment within the Soul

XXVI. Second Cause for Human-Beings Being Last: Avenging Justice for Unworthy Guests

Now this, then, is the First Cause for why the Human-Being appears to have been Generated for the sake of All-Things. But a Second Cause - though not without its own Aim - must also be declared. For when Humanity first came into Being, it found that all preparations for Life had already been made - clearly provided in advance, as though Nature herself were shouting aloud to those who came afterward: that if they would Imitate the First-Leader of the Human-Kind, they might pass through Life without toil or hardship, enjoying the most Abundant Wealth of all Necessary Things.

But this shall come to pass only if the Not-Rational Appetites - those twin Tyrannies of Gluttony and Lust, which seize control when the passions run unchecked - do not gain Dominion over the Life-Principle; and if the Desire for Glory, Wealth, or Power does not assert Sovereignty over one's Life; and if Sorrow does not Shrink and Twist the Mind, nor that wicked Counselor, Fear, suppress and hinder the Impulses that urge one toward Noble Deeds; nor if Folly, Cowardice, Injustice, or the innumerable and inescapable multitude of other Vices gain entrance.

For now, as all these have spread and flourished, Humanity has utterly abandoned itself to the Passions and to those Not-Restrained and Shameful Appetites, whose very Names it is Not-Lawful to Speak. And so, a fitting and Just-Judgment - an Avenging Justice for these Impious-Practices - confronts us all.

And this Justice is none other than the Difficulty in acquiring even the bare Necessities of Life. For only by laboriously cutting into the earth, channeling the streams of springs and rivers, scattering seeds, planting groves, and receiving the toil of the Farmers - unwearied by day and night, and repeated across the whole year - do human beings gather what is needed. And even then, these necessities often bring grief and prove insufficient, having been damaged by many harms: sometimes a succession of rains washes away the crops, or a sudden hailstorm crushes them entirely, or snow chokes them, or violent winds uproot them from their very roots. For Water and Air often conspire to bring Barren-Wasting upon the Fruits of the Earth.

But if the Not-Measured Impulses of the Passions could be restrained by Self-Control, and if the Injustices and Ambitions concerning Wrongful-Acts could be ruled by Justice, and - speaking simply - if Virtues and the Actualized-Activities in accordance with Virtue could prevail over Vices and the Ineffectual-Actions of Vice; if, in Truth, the War within the Soul - by far the most difficult and most grievous of all Wars - could be abolished; if Peace, following its cessation, could reign; and if that Peace, working through the Capacities within us, could prepare a condition of Order and Lawfulness, calm and serene - then there would be hope that the Jewish-God Himself, being a Lover of Virtue, a Lover of Beauty, and beyond this, a Lover of Humanity, would spontaneously and without delay bestow Good Things upon the Human-Kind, ready at hand.

For it is clear that it is far easier - without the Art of Farming - for the Jewish-God to draw forth what is needed from the Things that Already-Are, than for that which had not yet existed to be brought into Being from Non-Being.

XXVII. Third Cause for Human-Beings Being Last: Human-Beings are Completion of Heaven

Let the second Cause now be declared complete. The third is as follows: The Jewish-God, having determined to harmonize both the Origin and the Completion of all Generated Things - as those most Necessary and Most-Beloved - chose to establish the Heaven as the Origin, and the Human-Being as the Completion. The Heaven He made as the First among the Incorruptible and Apprehendable Things; the Human-

Being He placed as the Final and Best among the Earth-Born and Corruptible Beings.

And briefly stated - for the truth must be spoken - the Heaven, though vast, is compact in its composition: it bears within itself countless Star-Kinds, each a Sacred-Statue, and reveals countless Spectacles worthy of Song - marvels of Craft, Sciences, and every kind of Excellence.

But because the Corruptible and the Incorruptible are Opposed by Nature, the Jewish-God assigned the Most Beautiful of each Kind to their rightful place as Origin and Completion. The Origin, as has been said, He gave to the Heaven; the Completion, to the Human-Being.

XXVIII. Fourth Cause for Human-Beings Being Last: Awe, Submission, and Recognition from Other Living-Kinds

Yet beyond all else, this too must be stated, as the disclosure of a Necessary Cause: it was fitting that, after all other things had Come-Into-Being, the Human-Being should be the last to be Born - so that appearing suddenly and unexpectedly, he might strike astonishment into the Living-Kinds that had preceded him.

For he was destined to be seen and immediately inspire wonder - and even reverent submission - as though by

Nature he were a Ruler and Master. And so it was that all the other creatures, upon seeing him, were softened at once. Even the most savage of Natures, upon their very first encounter with the Human-Being, became most gentle, directing their ungovernable Rage and Wildness toward one another, but submitting tamely to him alone.

For this cause, the Father - having generated the Human as a Being-Ruling-by-Nature - not only gave him dominion in deed, but also formally appointed him, through a declaration of Rational-Language, as King over all things beneath the Moon: over those that dwell on land, in water, and in the air.

Whatever Mortal-Kinds inhabit the Three Elements - Earth, Water, and Air - the Jewish-God subordinated all of them to the Human. Only those Beings above the Heavens were excluded, as having been allotted a more Divine Share.

And the most evident proof of this Sovereignty is found in what is plainly observed: there are times when countless multitudes of Herd-Beasts are led by a single, chance Human - one who bears neither sword nor armor nor any instrument of defense, but only a simple covering of leather and a staff, which he carries either as a signal or to lean on during travel if weary.

Indeed, one sees that Shepherds, Goatherds, and Cowherds guide entire herds of sheep, goats, and oxen - Human-Beings who are neither physically strong nor vigorous, not men of overwhelming force, and certainly not awe-inspiring due to their health or stature.

Yet those vast and powerful herds - armed by Nature with strong limbs and natural defenses - stand before them like slaves before masters. They tremble, obey, and perform whatever is commanded.

Bulls are yoked to the plough and cut deep furrows in the soil by day, and sometimes even by night, as they stretch out long furrows under the eye of the supervising Farmer.

Rams, heavy with thick wool, especially in the springtime, respond calmly to the call of the Shepherd. Some even lie down in stillness, allowing themselves to be sheared, as though they were Citizens of a City offering their Annual Tribute to the King of Nature.

And even the most spirited creature - the Horse - is easily led once bridled, so that he does not rear or bolt, but lowers his back to receive the Rider's weight, bending himself into a posture well-suited to bearing the burden. Then, lifting the rider up and bearing him aloft, the Horse runs with great urgency, striving to reach whatever destination the rider commands. He arrives and conveys him there, while the rider, seated at ease and without toil, completes the journey with calm - by the strength and motion of another's Body and Feet.

XXIX. Fifth Cause for Human-Beings Being Last: Guide and Govern the Earthly Realm

One could speak of many additional matters, extending the account further, in order to show that nothing has been withheld or exempted from the Dominion of the Human-Being. But what has already been said is sufficient as Demonstration.

Nevertheless, this too must not be overlooked: the fact that the Human-Being came into Being last in the sequence does not imply inferiority in rank. Witnesses to this truth are the Charioteers and Ship-Pilots.

For charioteers, though they follow behind the yoked animals and move behind them along the path, nonetheless, whenever they choose, they direct the animals by means of the reins in their hands - sometimes letting them run freely in swift motion, at other times restraining them when their pace exceeds what is needed.

Likewise, the Pilots, having passed to the rearmost part of the ship - the Stern - are, as it were, the best and most skilled of all on board. For it is they who hold the safety of the ship and all within it in their own hands.

Just so, the Jewish-God fashioned the Human-Being as a kind of Charioteer and Pilot over all things under the Heavens. He appointed Humanity to Guide and Govern the Earthly Realm, taking charge of Living-Kinds - both Animals and Plants - as one entrusted with oversight by the First and Greatest King.

Part V: Moses Beyond Plato: The Jewish-God and the Hebdomad

XXX. Hebdomad: Jewish-God as Aesthetic Force

Now that the Whole Cosmos had been completed in accordance with the Number Six - which by Nature is Perfect - the Jewish-God, the Father, sanctified the Seventh Day. He praised it, named it Holy, and proclaimed it a Festival - not one limited to a single City or Country, but one belonging to the Whole. This Day alone is rightly called All-Public and truly deserves the name Birthday of the Cosmos.

As for the Nature of the Seventh - the Hebdomad - who could worthily hymn it? For it is beyond all Rational-Account. Yet we must not remain silent, as though such marvels should pass unspoken. Rather, we must dare to speak - even if not of all, nor of the highest things, but at least of those which are accessible to our understanding.

The Hebdomad is named in two ways. The first kind is within the Decad: it is composed of seven single units, each counted by the Monad alone - namely, 1+1+1+1+1+1+1.

The second kind is outside the Decad: it arises not from a series of units, but from Proportional-Numbers formed by doubling or tripling from the Monad, or by any numerical Ratio whatsoever - for instance, the numbers 64 and 729. The former (64) arises as the seventh in a doubling sequence from the Monad; the latter (729) as the seventh in a tripling sequence.

Each of these two kinds must be investigated, not superficially, but with care.

The second kind (the Proportional Hebdomad) displays a most evident preeminence. For in every Proportional Sequence - whether doubled, tripled, or otherwise - the Seventh Number will always be both a Square and a Cube, containing the Forms of both Bodiless and Bodily Substance.

For Square Numbers (formed from equal multiplications in two dimensions) correspond to the Plane and Bodiless Nature; while Cubic Numbers (formed in three dimensions) correspond to the Solid and Bodily Nature.

The Numbers already mentioned give clear proof of this:

The Seventh Number in the doubling sequence from the Monad is 64. It is a Square, being 8×8, and also a Cube, being 4×4×4.

Likewise, the Seventh Number in the tripling sequence from the Monad is 729. It is a Square, being 27×27, and also a Cube, being 9×9×9.

Indeed, anyone who makes the Seventh into a new starting point, and increases it proportionally, will always find that the Seventh in that new ratio will again be both a Square and a Cube.

For example: beginning from 64 and applying the doubling ratio again, the Seventh Number produced will be 4096, which is both a Square (with side 64) and a Cube (with side 16).

XXXI. Hebdomad: Another Kind (Decad)

We must now turn to the other kind of Hebdomad - the one contained within the Decad - which displays a marvelous structure and a Nature no less significant than the Proportional Hebdomad discussed earlier.

This form of Seven arises immediately from the combination of One, Two, and Four, which together contain two of the most harmonious ratios in all of Music and Number:

The 2:1 ratio, which corresponds to the Octave (διά πασῶν);

The 4:1 ratio, which corresponds to the Double Octave (δις διά πασῶν).

In addition, this Hebdomad includes other divisions, which - structured in a kind of Even-Coupling - display the inner symmetry of the Number Seven:

First, it divides into One and Six;

Then into Two and Five;

And finally into Three and Four.

These pairs reveal extraordinary Harmonic-Relations through their ratios:

Six to One produces the 6:1 ratio, the greatest interval in all Being. It marks the distance between the Highest Pitch and the Lowest Pitch - as we shall show more clearly when we turn from Number to the actual ratios found in Harmonic Music.

Five to Two reveals a great musical Power, nearly rivaling the force of the Octave itself. This is clearly demonstrated in canonical musical theory.

Four to Three gives us the First Harmony, known as the epitrite ratio (4:3), which constitutes the interval called the Fourth (διά τεσσάρων).

Thus, this internal form of the Hebdomad - constructed from foundational Numbers, interwoven through Music, Ratio, and Cosmic Order - reveals itself as the very Seed and Structure of Harmonic Being.

XXXII. Hebdomad: Triad and Tetrad

Another Form of Beauty is revealed within the Hebdomad - one that must be understood as Most-Sacred. For the Hebdomad, when composed from the Triad and the Tetrad, gives rise to what is by Nature Unbending and Upright among all Beings.

Let us now explain how.

The Right-Angled Triangle, which is the Archetype of Qualities, is composed from the Numbers Three, Four, and Five. Among these, the Three and the Four - which together constitute the very Substance of the Hebdomad - form the Right Angle itself.

For while the Obtuse and Acute Angles reveal the Irregular, the Disorderly, and the Unequal - since one is always more obtuse and the other more acute than another - the Right Angle admits of no such comparison. It does not allow for something to be more right than another; it remains constant in likeness to itself, never altering its Proper-Nature.

Now, if the Right-Angled Triangle is the Origin of Shapes and Qualities, and if the most Essential feature of that Triangle - the Right Angle - is generated by the Substance of the Hebdomad, that is, by the Triad and Tetrad, then it is entirely fitting to regard the Hebdomad as the Fountain and Source of all Form and of every Quality.

Moreover, to what has already been said, we may add another fitting reflection:

The Number Three corresponds to the Plane-Figure, since:

A Point belongs to the Monad,

A Line arises from the Dyad,

A Plane requires at minimum the Triad.

The Number Four, by adding Depth to the Plane, gives rise to the Solid Body.

From this, it is evident that the Substance of the Hebdomad - composed of Three and Four - is the Beginning of both Geometry and Solid Geometry, and, to put it most concisely, it is the Origin of both the Bodiless and the Bodied Realms.

XXXIII. Hebdomad (Unique-Status of Sacred-Dignity)
So profound is the Sacred-Dignity embedded within the Hebdomad that it holds a Unique-Status apart from all the Numbers contained within the Decad. Among those other numbers:

Some are Generating but not Generated;

Others are Generated but do not Generate;

Still others Both Generate and Are Generated.

But the Hebdomad (Seven) alone is observed to be neither. This claim must be confirmed by demonstration.

The Number One generates all subsequent numbers but is itself generated by nothing.

The Number Eight is generated by the double of Four (2×4) but does not generate any other number within the Decad.

The Number Four fulfills both roles: it generates Eight (2×4) and is generated by Two (2×2).

But Seven, as stated, is the only number that neither generates nor is generated.

Because of this, many Philosophers liken the Hebdomad to the figure of Victory Unmothered and Virgin-Born - that one whom myth says sprang forth from the head of Zeus.

The Pythagoreans, for their part, liken the Hebdomad to the Leader and Ruler of All. For that which neither generates nor is generated must remain Unmoving. And Generation, by its very nature, is bound up with Motion: for the one who generates must move in order to generate, and the one who is generated must be moved in order to come into being.

But only that which neither moves nor is moved - namely, the Elder Ruler and Supreme Governor - could be aptly named the True-Image of the Hebdomad.

And as a witness to this Logos, Philolaus also proclaims:

"The Jewish-God is the Ruler and Governor of All. Being Eternal, Immovable, Unchanging, and Like unto Himself, He is wholly Other than all created things."

XXXIV. Hebdomad (Apprehendable-Realm)
In the Intelligible-Realm, the Hebdomad reveals itself as that which is Unmoving and Unaffected. But in the Apprehendable-Realm, it demonstrates a Great and Most-Binding Power - a power by which all Earthly Things are brought to Fulfillment, especially as seen in the Cycles of the Moon.

Let us now examine how this occurs.

The Number Seven, composed in sequence from the Monad, generates the Number Twenty-Eight - a Perfect Number that is equal to the sum of its own parts. And this number, in turn, is the Restorative Number of the Moon.

From the moment the Moon begins to acquire visible shape, it increases over the course of seven days, from its first crescent until it reaches the half-moon (dichotomy). Then, in another seven days, it becomes full (plenilune). Thereafter, it begins to decrease, reversing its path:

From full moon back to half-moon in seven days;

From half-moon back to crescent, again in seven days.

Thus, the full lunar cycle is fulfilled in the Number Twenty-Eight, composed of four phases of seven days.

Because of this power of Fulfillment, the Hebdomad is called by those most precise in their naming: Telēsphoros - Bringer of Completion. For it is by means of this number that All Things reach their Telos (Completion).

This may also be demonstrated through the structure of the Organic Body, which makes use of:

Three Dimensions: length, breadth, and depth;

Four Boundaries: point, line, surface, and solid.

The combination of these (three + four) results in the Hebdomad.

It would be impossible for Bodies to be measured by the Hebdomad in this manner - by combining the three Dimensions and the four Boundaries - unless the Ideas of the first Numbers (One, Two, Three, and Four), which lay the foundation of the Decad, were also found to contain the Nature of the Hebdomad.

These four Numbers have:

Four Terms: first, second, third, and fourth;

And they imply three Transitions:

From One to Two;

From Two to Three;

From Three to Four.

Thus, the Hebdomad, arising from this triadic progression through four terms, is revealed once again as the Binding-Unity at the heart of both Geometry and Kosmic Completion.

XXXV. Hebdomad (Ages of Human-Life)

The clearest testimony to the Power of Completion contained in the Hebdomad may be found in the Ages of Human Life - from Infancy to Old Age - which are measured precisely according to this Sacred Number.

In the first Hebdomad (1–7), the emergence of Teeth marks the bodily beginning.

In the second Hebdomad (8–14), one becomes capable of Releasing Generative Seed.

In the third Hebdomad (15–21), the Beard begins to grow, signaling the bloom of Masculine Form.

In the fourth Hebdomad (22–28), there is a Strengthening of Body and vital energy.

The fifth Hebdomad (29–35) is the Time of Marriage, and the beginning of seeking offspring.

The sixth Hebdomad (36–42) is the Peak of Intelligence and Rational Mastery.

In the seventh Hebdomad (43–49), there is a dual Perfection of Mind and Speech, growing together in harmony.

The eighth Hebdomad (50–56) brings about the Completion of both faculties - Mind and Logos - at their highest point.

In the ninth Hebdomad (57–63), the Passions begin to Soften, and Moderation and Mildness characterize the Soul.

The tenth Hebdomad (64–70), if completed according to its Measure, marks the Desirable End of Life, when the Bodily Organs are still intact - though Old Age, ever the subtle adversary, seeks to undermine and dissolve each part.

These Life-Measures were also recorded by Solon, the Lawgiver of Athens, who rendered them in elegiac verse:

"As a Child, not yet pubescent,
the infant casts out its first line of teeth in the first Seven years.

In the next Seven, signs of ripening Youth appear,
as the Jewish-God brings forth growth.

By the third Hebdomad, soft hair adorns the limbs,
as color changes and Manhood awakens.

In the fourth Hebdomad, Strength stands at its peak,
and Virtue marks the form of the mature Man.

The fifth Hebdomad calls one to Marriage,
to seek out future Generations.

In the sixth, the Mind is fully trained

and no longer seeks unlawful Deeds.

In the seventh Hebdomad,
both Reason and Speech attain their height.

The eighth fulfills both of these again,
four times two, and ten besides.

In the ninth, the Soul softens,
but grows ever nearer to True Virtue -
Mind and Speech are now well-formed.

And if one should reach the tenth in due measure,
his Death would come not as a curse,
but as a fitting end in accordance with Nature."

XXXVI. Hebdomad (Solon and Hippocrates)

Solon, the Lawgiver, numbered the span of human life by ten sets of Seven, while Hippocrates the Physician declared that there are seven distinct Ages of a Human-Being: that of the Infant, the Child, the Youth, the Young Man, the Man, the Elder, and the Old Man. These stages, though counted by Sevens, do not follow strictly in identical sequence. He speaks thus: "In the Nature of the Human there are seven Seasons, which are called Ages: Infant, Child, Youth, Young Man, Man, Elder, and Old Man. The Infant lasts until the age of seven years and the falling out of the first teeth. The Child remains until the emergence of seed, reaching to the second Seven. The Youth extends to the sprouting of the beard, completing the third Seven. The Young Man endures until the full expansion of the Body, reaching the fourth Seven. The Man stretches on until the fiftieth year, the seventh Seven. The Elder continues to fifty-six, the eighth Seven. And what lies beyond is the stage of the Old Man."

And this too is rightly said for the purpose of disclosing the inherent harmony of the Hebdomad - the Sevenfold Principle - which holds wondrous Order within Nature. For the Number Seven is composed of Three and Four. The Third Number from the Monad (One), if doubled, becomes a Square; the Fourth becomes a Cube. The Sixth, arising from both, becomes simultaneously a Cube and a Square. The Third Number, in a double proportion, is Four - a perfect Square. The Fourth is Eight - a perfect Cube. The Seventh, being Four added to Sixty, becomes both Cube and Square, a symbol of completeness, announcing through its dual equality both the Flatness of the Square (by its kinship with Three) and the Solidity of the Cube (through its relation to Four). Thus is the Hebdomad, composed of Three and Four, a Perfect Number.

XXXVII. Hebdomad (Fountain of the Most Beautiful Diagram)

This Number Seven, then, is not only Complete but, one might truly say, the most Harmonious of all - and in some sense, the very Fountain of the Most Beautiful Diagram. It contains, as if by nature, the totality of all Harmonic Intervals: the Harmony in Fourths, the Harmony in Fifths, and the Full Harmony of All. And likewise, it embraces all Proportions: the Numerical, the Geometrical, and the Harmonic.

This Harmonious Diagram, this Divine Brick, is composed of the numbers Six, Eight, Nine, and Twelve. The Eight compared to the Six stands in the ratio of a Third (epitritos), which is the foundation of the Harmony in Fourths. The Nine compared to the Six stands in the ratio of a Half and a Half (hemiolios), which is the Harmony in Fifths. And the Twelve to the Six is in the Double Ratio, which corresponds to the Harmony of the Whole.

Moreover, as has been said, these numbers contain all types of Proportion. The Arithmetic Proportion is manifest in Six, Nine, and Twelve: for just as Nine exceeds Six by Three, so does Twelve exceed Nine by Three. The Geometric Proportion is found in the Fourfold Set: as Eight is to Six, so is Twelve to Nine - the ratio being a Third. And the Harmonic Proportion appears in the triplet Six, Eight, and Twelve.

Now the judgment of Harmonic Proportion is twofold. First, when the Last Number bears to the First a ratio equal to the surplus by which it exceeds the Middle, and likewise, the First is exceeded by the Middle by that same surplus. One will see this quite clearly in the numbers just given - Six, Eight, and Twelve. For Twelve is double Six, and the surplus is also doubled: Twelve exceeds Eight by Four, and Eight exceeds Six by Two - again, a doubling.

There is also another test of Harmonic Proportion: when the Middle Number both exceeds and is exceeded by the Extremes by equal fractional parts. Here, again, Eight is the Middle between Six and Twelve. It exceeds Six by one-third (for removing Six from Eight leaves Two, which is one-third of Six) and is exceeded by Twelve in the same way (for removing Eight from Twelve leaves Four, which is one-third of Twelve). Thus, the Harmony is verified both by doubling and by equal fractional difference, and all things rejoice in the Mystery of the Number Seven and its sacred offspring.

XXXVIII. Hebdomad (Cosmos)

Let all this, then, be stated in reverence for the grandeur of that Diagram - whether one calls it the Sacred Brick or gives it another fitting name. For the Heptad reveals within itself such a multitude of Forms, and even more beyond, in the Incorporeal and Intelligible realm. Yet the Nature of this Sacred Seven extends beyond the Unseen, permeating all the Visible Substance as well - reaching up to Heaven, down to Earth, and out to the farthest Boundaries of the All.

For what part of the Cosmos is not seized by desire and longing for the Heptad? Consider first the Heavens: they are said to be girded by seven Circles - whose names are as follows: the Arctic Circle, the Antarctic, the Summer Tropic, the Winter Tropic, the Equinoctial, the Zodiacal, and in addition, the Milky Way. The Horizon too, though it appears a fixed boundary, is in fact a passion of our own perception. Depending on whether one's vision is sharp or dull, the line of sight shifts - sometimes tracing a narrower, sometimes a broader circumference.

And then the Planets - the Counter-Marching Host opposed to the Fixed-Stars - are organized into Seven Orders, showing extraordinary sympathy with Air and Earth. By their movements, they call forth the Seasons, and in each moment they bring about a thousand changes: calm skies, clear weather, cloudings, violent outbursts of wind. Rivers rise or shrink; plains become lakes, and lakes, again, disappear. Even the seas obey these heavenly governors: the tides reverse course or swell into surges. There are times when gulfs draw back under the force of ebbing tides, revealing shoals deep enough to walk; and then, soon after, come great floods that transform those shallows into the deepest ocean -

now fit for no petty boats, but for great cargo-laden ships.

As for all Earthly things - animals and plants alike - they too are governed by the Seven: in the generation of fruit, in their growth and in their ripening, they follow long circuits inscribed into their Nature, blossoming in old age and bearing to fullness in order to bestow abundant provision upon all in need.

XXXIX. Hebdomad (Star Constellations)

Now consider also the Bear - the constellation which is said to be the guide and herald of seafarers. It consists of seven stars, and upon it the helmsmen fix their gaze as they cut across the infinite paths of the sea. A marvel, indeed - a deed more astonishing than what human nature alone could aspire to. For by tracing the wandering patterns of those Seven Lights, they uncovered lands formerly unknown: islands by those dwelling on continents, continents by those dwelling on islands. For it was necessary, beneath the most radiant Heaven - the substance clearest and most divine - that the hidden recesses of Earth and Sea be unveiled to the race of man, that living being most beloved by God.

In addition to these, consider the chorus of the Pleiades: a gathering of stars completed also in the number Seven. Their risings and settings bring forth great blessings for all. When they disappear below the horizon, the furrows of the fields are plowed for sowing. And when they rise again, they announce the time of harvest. Upon their appearance, the joyful farmer is stirred to gather the necessary provisions, and with gladness lays up nourishment for daily use.

Moreover, the great Ruler of the Day - the Sun - confirms this sacred seventh principle as well. For twice each year, he establishes an Equinox: once in the Spring, in the sign of Aries, and once in the Autumn, in the sign of Libra. Each occurs, as a most visible testimony, in the seventh month. And it is precisely in those months, ordained by law, that the most sacred and widely celebrated Festivals are held. For in both seasons, the fruits of the Earth reach completion: in Spring, the wheat and all that is sown; in Autumn, the grape and the great multitude of fruit-bearing trees.

XL. Hebdomad (Human Soul, Body, Head)

Now, since earthly things are bound to the heavenly by a certain natural Sympathy, the principle of the Seventh - having begun its journey above - descends downward and enters even into us mortals at the moment of our coming-into-being.

First of all, the Soul within us is parted, beneath its governing part, into Seven: five are the Sense-Apprehensions, the sixth is the Voice-Producing Organ, and the seventh is the Generative Power. These seven - like marvels on strings - are all governed by the leading Principle, which, like a Puppeteer, now calms and now excites each function according to its fitting rhythm and movement.

Likewise, if one were to examine the body, both in its external and internal regions, again one would find the number Seven. Externally: the Head, the Chest, the Belly, the two Hands, and the two Feet - seven in total. Internally, the organs commonly called Entrails are also seven: the Stomach, the Heart, the Lungs, the Spleen, the Liver, and the two Kidneys.

Once more, the most Sovereign part in a living being - the Head - makes use of precisely seven essential members: two Eyes, two Ears, two Nostrils, and the Mouth as the seventh. Through this Mouth occurs both entrance and exit - entrance for mortal nourishment, as Plato said, and exit for what belongs to the immortal. For through this opening, food and drink enter - mortal sustenance for the mortal body - whereas Words pass out: immortal Laws for the immortal Soul. By these, the rational life is rightly governed.

XLI. Hebdomad (Physicality and Hippocrates)

The things judged through the noblest of the Sense-Apprehensions - namely, Sight - also participate in the principle of Number by kind, for there are Seven visible phenomena: Body, Extension, Shape, Magnitude, Color, Motion, and Rest. Beyond these, nothing further can be seen.

Likewise, the Modulations of Voice are said to be Seven in number: the Acute, the Grave, the Circumflex, the Rough Sound as fourth, the Smooth as fifth, the Long as sixth, and the Short as seventh.

Moreover, there are also said to be Seven Movements: Upward, Downward, to the Right, to the Left, Forward, Backward, and Circular - these being especially observable in those who exhibit their art in Dancing.

It is also declared that the Expulsions from the Body are arranged under the same sacred Number. For through the Eyes flow Tears; through the Nostrils, purgations from the Head; through the Mouth, spittle is discharged. Then there are two outlets provided for the evacuation of excrements - one anterior and one posterior. A sixth is the profuse Sweat that is emitted from the whole body. The Seventh, most according to Nature, is the emission of Seed through the Generative Organs.

It is also said by Hippocrates - the one most experienced in discerning Nature - that both the coagulation of seed and the reconstruction of flesh are established within a period of Seven days. Again, in women, the periodic flow occurs most often in cycles of Seven days. And the generation of children in the womb is completed, as Nature intends, within Seven months. This, though astonishing, is true: for Seven-month births are viable, whereas those born in the Eighth month, as a rule, do not live.

Even the gravest illnesses of the body - especially when continuous fevers arise from the imbalance of inner powers - most often reach a decisive turn on the Seventh day. For this day delivers a Judgment in the contest for the Life-Principle: to some it grants Salvation, to others, Death.

XLII. Hebdomad (Grammar and Music)
The Power of the Sacred Seven has not only appeared in the phenomena already named, but it has also descended into the noblest of the Sciences - Grammar and Music.

The Seven-Stringed Lyre, for instance, harmonizing with the dance of the Seven Wandering-Stars, completes the Rational Harmonies and serves as something like the Guiding-Form of the entire craft of Instrumental-Music.

As for the Letters in the science of Grammar, the so-called Vowels are, rightly, Seven in number - since they seem to produce Sound by themselves, and, when joined with other elements, generate Articulated Voice. Among the Semi-Vocal sounds, the Vowel supplies what is lacking, thereby completing the Whole Tones. Among the Mute sounds, it transforms and alters their natures by infusing its own Force, so that what is Unspeakable may become Speakable.

For this reason, it seems to me that those Wise Ones who from the beginning named things according to their Natures also named the Number Seven from the reverence and solemn dignity associated with it.

And the Romans, adding the one Element which the Greeks had left out - the Letter "S" - have with even greater emphasis revealed the significance of this sacred Number. For they call it septem, a name more truly derived from semeness and reverence, as has just been explained.

XLIII. Hebdomad (Exalted by Moses Above All Other Law-Givers)

Much more is said and deeply contemplated by the Philosophers concerning the Sacred Seven. For this reason, it has attained the Highest Honors within Nature herself, and it has also been held in esteem by the most distinguished among both Greeks and Barbarians - especially by those who labor in the discipline of Mathematical Science.

Yet above all, it was exalted by the Virtue-Lover Moses, who inscribed the Beauty of this Number upon the Holiest Tablets of the Law. And not only there: he engraved it also into the Minds of all under his guidance, commanding that every Seventh Day be set apart as Sacred.

On that day, one was to abstain from all labor done for livelihood or acquisition, and instead devote oneself wholly to Philosophic Contemplation - aimed at the Refinement of Moral Character and the Examination of Conscience.

This Conscience, implanted deep within the Soul like a Judge, rebukes without partiality: sometimes with stern threats, other times with gentler admonitions depending on whether the transgression arose from Deliberate Injustice, in which case it is met with harsh warning, or from Ignorance and Lack of Foresight, in which case it is met with mild correction. In both cases, the purpose is the same: that the Soul may no longer slip into Error as before.

Part VI: Moses Beyond Plato: the The Life-Principle, Internal-Judgment, and Sense-Apprehensions

XLIV. Moses' Compressed Formulation

Reflecting upon the making of the Cosmos, the Sacred Narrative presents a compressed formulation, declaring: "This is the scroll of the genesis of Heaven and Earth, when they came-to-be, on the day when the Jewish-God made the Heaven and the Earth, and every sprout of the field before it was in the earth, and every herb of the field before it sprang up" (Genesis 2:4–5).

Does this not clearly present the Incorporeal and Intelligible Forms, which have become, as it were, the Seals of Sensible Results? For before the Earth sprouted greenery, that very Greenery already existed - in the Nature of Realities themselves, it says. And before any visible Herb sprang up from the Field, there was already Herbness, though not yet perceptible.

One must grasp that for each perceptible thing, the ruling powers of Sense-Perception bear witness to their elder Forms and Measures. By these, all that comes-to-be is given shape and scale - and these existed beforehand.

And indeed, even if the Divine Narrative did not proceed part by part but revealed all things in a single gathered

Vision - still, even in its brevity, what has been said stands as a token of the Whole of Nature. And Nature, in turn, produces nothing in the realm of Sense without an Incorporeal Archetype by which it is accomplished.

XLV. Moses' Unique Contribution: Fresh-Water Distinct From Salt-Water

Following the ordered progression and preserving the harmonious linkage of what comes after to what came before, the Sacred Account continues: "And a spring would ascend from the earth and water the whole face of the ground" (Genesis 2:6).

The other philosophers declared water to be one of the four Elements - indeed, to be the primal one from which the Cosmos was composed. But Moses, whose sight was sharper and whose vision was accustomed to range far and clearly, judged differently. He considered the vast Sea to be an Element - not merely a part, but a fourth portion of the Whole - and this is what later thinkers named Ocean, believing that the navigable seas near us were but its harbors.

But the Sweet and Drinkable water, Moses distinguished from the sea's salty depths. He assigned it instead to the Earth, counting it as part of Her rather than of Ocean. And the reason he gives is wise: the Sweetness of this water, like a binding glue, coheres with the Earth as if joined by a bond. For if the Earth were left dry, without moisture filtering up through its loosened pores, it would dissolve into powder.

What holds it together and sustains it is, first, the power of unifying Breath; and second, the nature of the Moist Element itself, which refuses to allow the Earth to collapse into dust, instead binding even the smallest clods with invisible adhesion.

This is one reason. But another may also be offered, drawn like an arrow toward the target of truth: nothing born of Earth comes into Being without the presence of Moisture. The very nature of Seeds reveals this, since they are moist substances. This is true for animals, whose seed cannot generate without moisture; and it is likewise true for plants.

From this it is clear that the Moist Essence must be considered part of the Earth - the All-Mother of all Generation - just as in women the flow of menstrual blood is said by some natural philosophers to be a bodily substance, material for the child to grow from.

And this understanding is not inconsistent with what is still to be revealed. For to every mother, Nature has given breasts as a most necessary feature, preparing nourishment beforehand for the child about to be born.

And so, too, the Earth - who is most ancient and most fertile of all Mothers - was deemed worthy by Nature to bear, as if breasts, the flowing streams of rivers and fountains, so that both plants might be watered and every animal have abundant drink.

XLVI. Breath of Life

After these things, it is said: "And the Jewish-God formed the Human by shaping dust taken from the Earth, and He breathed into his face the Breath of Life" (Gen. 2:7). With this, the distinction could not be clearer: there exists an immense and essential difference between this now-shaped Human and the one previously made according to the Image of the Jewish-God.

For the Human shaped now is perceptible - already mingled with qualities, composed of Body and Life-Principle, whether male or female by nature, and mortal by design.

But the one made in the Image was not of this kind - it was an Idea, a Form-Kind, a Seal: intelligible, bodiless, neither male nor female, incorruptible by its very nature.

As for the now-visible and individuated Human, his construction is said to be a Compound - drawn from both the Earthy Substance and the Divine-Breath.

The Body came into being from the dust, molded by the Artisan's hand and shaped into Human-Form.

But the Life-Principle was not generated from any created source at all. It was drawn from the Father and Sovereign of All:

For He breathed in - and what was this if not Divine-Breath itself? A colony sent forth from that Blessed and Happy Nature above, implanted here below for the benefit of our kind, so that even though the Human is mortal by his visible portion, he might be rendered immortal by his invisible share.

Thus it is most fitting to say:

The Human is a border-being - standing between Mortal and Immortal Nature, participating necessarily in both, and brought into being as a creature both mortal and immortal:

Mortal according to the Body; Immortal according to the Mind.

XLVII. First Human (Earth-Born and Origin-Leader)

That First Human - Earth-born and Origin-Leader of our entire kind - appears to me to have been fashioned as the best in both Life-Principle and Body, surpassing by far all who came after him in the excess of both aspects.

For in truth, this one was beautiful and good in the highest sense.

One could demonstrate the excellence of his bodily form through three clear proofs:

First, the Earth itself, having only just appeared following the separation from the vast Waters - which were gathered together and named the Sea - still possessed its substance in an unmingled, unpolluted, and pristine condition.
The Material out of which beings were shaped was still pure, without corruption, still yielding and noble - so that what came forth from it could be formed blamelessly.

Second, it does not seem that the Jewish-God took dust at random from just any part of the Earth when forming this Human-shaped image.
Rather, with the utmost care and selection, He chose the finest portion from the whole Earth - the most refined, the most purified, the best of the pure Material - perfectly suited for the construction at hand.

For what was being built was not merely a dwelling, but a sacred temple for the Rational Life-Principle, which would come to inhabit this body as its most divine Image-Bearer.

Third - though it is in no way comparable to the prior reasons - the Artisan Himself was Good, in all respects and in knowledge.

He assigned precise numbers to each part of the body, crafting every limb and organ with numerical harmony, so that each individual piece was proportioned in perfect relation to the whole.

To this symmetry He added well-formed flesh and radiant complexion, painting it with harmonious color, wishing - as far as was possible - for the First Human to be seen as the most Beautiful.

XLVIII. First Human's Life-Principle (Divine-Logos)

That the First Human's Life-Principle was also the most excellent is evident - for in crafting it, the Jewish-God drew upon no model from among the things already generated.

Instead, He shaped it after only one Pattern: His own Divine-Logos.

Thus, He declares that this Human was an Image-Impression and a Likeness of that Divine-Logos - having been breathed into the face, where the Apprehensive-Senses dwell.

Through these Apprehensions the Artisan endowed the Body with vitality, and He established the Sovereign Reasoning-Capacity to rule from the Command-Center of the soul.

This Sovereign-Capacity was assigned to govern and interpret all influxes of colors, sounds, liquors, vapors, and similar perceptions - none of which could be comprehended except through Sense-Apprehension, which acts as the intermediary.

Now, it necessarily follows that a Pattern of absolute Beauty will produce an image of corresponding Beauty.

And since the Divine-Logos of the Jewish-God is not merely beautiful, but is Beauty-Itself in Nature - greater than any beauty which is externally adorned -
the Divine-Logos is not ornamented with Beauty; rather, it is Ornament and Order Itself.
Indeed, if we must speak the truth: it is the True Cosmos, more radiant than even the visible cosmos.
XLIX. First Human (Surpassed all Those Who Came Before Us)

Such, then, was the First Human, both in Body and in Life-Principle - a being who surpassed not only all those alive now, but also all who came before us.

For our own coming-into-being arises from other humans -

but that First One was fashioned directly by the Jewish-God.

And inasmuch as the Artisan is superior to those He creates, by just that measure, too, is His creation nobler than what comes after.

Just as the prime of life is more vigorous than what follows its decline - whether it be in animal, plant, fruit, or any other being found in Nature -

so too, the First Human appears as the climactic-peak of the entire human race.

Those who came after him could never again reach such flourishing, but instead inherited faded forms and weakened powers -

just as in the arts of sculpture or painting, each copy is a step removed from the Original-Pattern.

And if one draws not from the Archetype but from a copy-of-a-copy, the result becomes ever more degraded, increasingly distant from the Source.

Something similar is demonstrated in the Magnet-Stone:
Of the iron rings it holds in suspension, the one it touches directly is seized most powerfully.
The second ring, held by the first, is drawn less firmly.
A third hangs from the second, a fourth from the third, and so on down the chain - each link held by the fading force of the one before it.
But as they recede further from the Source, they begin to weaken and sag, for the Attracting-Force can no longer bind them with equal strength.

So too does it seem that the human race has suffered the same condition:
With each generation, the powers and qualities of both Body and Life-Principle have dimmed and grown less vivid.

Thus, to call that Primal Founder not only the First Human, but the Only True Citizen-of-the-Cosmos, would be no falsehood.

For the entire Cosmos was his dwelling and his city - he required no man-made structure assembled from stone or timber.
Rather, as if in his ancestral homeland, he lived secure and untroubled,

free from fear, since he had been appointed Ruler over all the Earthly Beings,

and all mortal creatures, having been struck with awe, were taught - or compelled - to obey him as Master.

He lived, then, in peaceful Delight-without-War, moving freely within the Joy of Rest.

L. Citizen-of-the-Cosmos Lives by Right-Reason of Nature

Now, since every well-governed City must possess a Constitution, it necessarily followed that the Citizen-of-the-Cosmos should live according to the Constitution of the Cosmos itself.

And this Constitution is none other than the Right-Reason of Nature -
which, in its truest name, is called Statute: a Divine Law.
By this Law, all things have been assigned their due and proper share -
and all beings have been apportioned their roles and obligations.

Thus, even before the coming of the human citizen, this Cosmic City required inhabitants -
and rightly might we call them Great-Citizens,

for they dwell within the widest of Perimeters and are inscribed into the most Perfect of Polities.

And who are these Citizens?
Surely none but the Rational and Divine Natures -
some incorporeal and intelligible, others not without bodies,
such as the Stars, who appear to participate in the Laws of Reason.

With such beings did the First Human dwell, converse, and share his life -
spending his days in unmixed Blessedness,
for he was of kindred seed and near lineage to the Sovereign-Mind,
having received into himself a vast outpouring of the Divine-Breath.

All his words and deeds were directed toward the delight of his Father and King,
and he followed the path of that Sovereign as closely as one might trace a footprint in the earth.

Those Paths, rightly called Royal Roads,
are carved through the Cosmos by the Virtues -
and only Souls, aiming at their End, are permitted to walk them.

For the End is this: Likeness to the Jewish-God who Generated them.

Part VII: Moses Beyond Plato: Internal-Judgment and Cosmos-Citizens

LI. Twofold Binding Joining Humans to Cosmos and Divine

As for the First Human, the one planted into Being by Divine Hands, the account has already traced, in terms befitting our mortal limitations, the dual Beauty of his Soul and Body - though it must be confessed, such a depiction inevitably falls far short of the full Measure of Truth. Yet even so, among his descendants there remains, however dimly, the imprint of that original Form. For it is necessary that all who spring from that Primal Stock preserve at least the faint outlines, the faded stamp, of their kinship to the Ancestor who first bore the Divine Shape.

And what is this kinship, if not the twofold binding that joins all humans both to the cosmos and to the Divine? In Mind, every human is closely tied to the Divine-Logos, as though fashioned from a cast of the Blessed Nature - an image, a fragment, a radiant echo of its Source. In Body, the human is made kin to the Whole Living Cosmos, being composed from the very same elemental substratum - earth and water, air and fire - each of which contributes its due share, so that the sum might be a complete and self-sufficient material, worthy to be seized by the Artisan's hand for the shaping of this visible image, this microcosm of life.

Nor is this kinship merely structural - it is also experiential. For the human dwells amid all the realms of nature as if they were native homes: sometimes anchored to the soil, sometimes cast upon the seas, sometimes lifted by the breath of air, and sometimes even ascending in vision to the stars. Thus rightly might one say: the human is all things - dweller of land, of water, of air, and even of heaven. For he walks upon the earth like a terrestrial beast; he sails and swims like one born for the waters, as is evident in the lives of merchants, sailors, divers, and all who draw sustenance from the sea; he is carried aloft by nature, raised up from the ground like a winged creature of the air; and through the sovereign power of Sight - the most ruling of all the senses - he communes with the sun and moon, draws near to the planets and the fixed stars, and finds kinship even with the heavenly lights.

LII. Task of Naming (Governor of All Living Beings)

Rightly and with divine fitness was the task of naming entrusted to the First-Formed Man (Genesis 2:19). For such an act belongs to both Wisdom and Kingship - and this First Man was both: wise by nature, taught not by others but self-taught and self-instructed, having been formed by the hands of God. Moreover, he was a King. It is indeed fitting for a true Ruler to assign names to each of his subjects.

And rightly so - for a surpassing degree of Rule and Sovereignty surrounded that original Man, whom the Jewish-God had shaped with divine seriousness and judged worthy of the world's stewardship: belonging to Himself, but set above all others as Governor of All Living Beings. This is why even those born many generations later, far removed through the long circuit of Time from the origin, still retain dominion over the Non-Rational Living Kinds. As if bearing a torch of Rulership handed down from the first human, they still hold sway, guarding the original transmission of Sovereign Power.

The text says that the Jewish-God brought every Living Kind before Adam, not because He was unsure what name would be given - nothing is unknown to God - but because He had implanted in the Mortal Nature a Rational Capacity that moves of its own accord. God, Himself untouched by Evil, set forth as Guide and Examiner this inner power, rousing within Adam the latent habit of speech and calling forth the articulation of thought through action. The goal was that he might name each thing not at random, nor with misfit terms, but with designations that clearly reflected the distinctive Essence of Each Being.

For at that time, Rational Nature was still untainted in the Life-Principle: no sickness, no weakness, no inner disturbance had yet intruded. Thus, he received the impressions of bodies and beings in their purest clarity, and from that undistorted apprehension, he fashioned names with exactness. His speech aimed truly at the mark, and his naming was both direct and luminous, as if each word unveiled the very nature of the thing named.

And so, in this too, did the First Man distinguish himself - reaching the height of Human Blessedness, and suffering no envy in its perfection.

LIII. Woman and Misfortune

Since nothing that enters into the realm of Becoming can remain stable - since all Mortal things must, by their nature, undergo changes and transformations - it was inevitable that even the First Man would taste some form of Misfortune. And the beginning of his Mortal-Accountable Life came through the creation of Woman.

For as long as he remained alone, he resembled, in that Solitary Condition, both Cosmos and God - and his Life-

Principle bore within itself the Imprints of both Natures, receiving as many Divine-Marks as a Mortal Composition could possibly contain. But once Woman was fashioned, and he beheld a kindred form, a brother-like image, he was gladdened by the sight. Approaching her, he welcomed her with joy.

She, too, seeing in him the one creature most akin and resembling herself, was delighted and returned his address with modesty and recognition. And then came Eros - Love and Longing - binding these two halves of what had once been one Living Being, now separated but drawn back together. This Desire, settling in each for the other, drew them into Union, not merely of bodies, but toward the shared Generation of the Same Kind.

But this Desire, in joining their bodies, also brought into being Bodily Pleasure, which is the seed and starting-point of Injustice and Lawlessness. For through it, they were exchanged away - traded out of the Immortal and Blessed Life into the Mortal and Ill-Fated One.

LIV. Garden of Paradise

Before the formation of Woman, while the First Man still lived a Solitary Life, it is said that the Jewish-God planted a Paradise - a Garden unlike anything known among us (Gen. ii. 8ff). What we call "gardens" are lifeless material spaces, filled with a variety of trees: some evergreen, offering undiminished pleasure, like that which tempts the Serpent; others that bloom only with the Spring Seasons, bearing fruits in cycles. Some of these bear gentle fruits for human beings - not only for necessary sustenance, but also for excessive enjoyment, fitting for a luxurious way of life. Others bear fruits not suited to us, and are thus rightly granted to beasts.

But the Divine Paradise is altogether different. Here, each plant is ensouled and rational, bearing as fruit the Virtues: Incorruptible Understanding, Sharp Discernment, which knows the Beautiful and the Shameful, Unafflicted Life, Immortality, and all things kindred to these.

These things, I believe, are spoken symbolically rather than literally. For no trees of Life or Understanding have ever grown upon the Earth, nor is it likely that they ever will. Rather, what is hinted at is this: by Paradise, we are to understand the Ruling-Part of the Soul, which is overflowing - like a grove of countless plants - with Opinions and Appearances.

The Tree of Life signifies the Greatest of Virtues, which is Reverence for the Divine - for through this, the Life-Principle is made Immortal. The Tree of Knowledge of

Good and Evil, by contrast, represents Practical Discernment, that Middle-Region of Reason by which things of opposite nature are distinguished.

LV. Divine and the Boundaries within the Soul

Having established these Boundaries within the Soul - as if seated as a Judge - the Divine observed which way the Soul would incline. And seeing her tilting toward Cunning and turning away from Reverence and Holiness - those very Powers through which Immortal Life is attained - the Maker responded according to Justice: He banished her from Paradise, denying the Soul, now wounded beyond cure, even the hope of return.

This act was not without just cause, and the pretext of her error cannot pass in silence. It is said that in olden times, that poisonous, earth-born crawling creature - the Serpent - emitted human speech. Once, it is told, it approached the Woman, who had been formed from the First-Man, and reproached her for her hesitation and excessive caution, accusing her of delaying in enjoying the most beautiful and delightful of fruits.

It praised the fruit not only for its pleasure, but for its usefulness, claiming it would grant her the Power to Know both Good and Evil. And so, without examination, relying on a judgment unrooted and uncertain, she consented and ate - and offered it also to the Man. And so suddenly, both were transformed: from their previous innocence and simplicity of character, they shifted into Craftiness.

In doing so, they provoked the wrath of the Father - for the deed was worthy of Judgment. They had bypassed the Tree of Immortal Life, the Complete Perfection of Virtue, through which they could have harvested a long, blessed life, and instead chose a path not truly worthy of being called Life, but rather a time filled with Misery, fleeting and mortal.

Thus, the just punishments for their actions were assigned in accordance with their deeds.

LVI. Not Sophism or Myth but Allegorical Insight

These things, then, are not the fabrications of mere myth, of the sort that delights the poetic or sophistic mind. Rather, they are Symbolic Tokens, summoning us toward Allegorical Insight, to be interpreted according to the method of hidden meanings. One who follows a reasonable line of interpretation may rightly say that the Serpent is the Emblem of Pleasure.

For, first of all, it is a creature without feet, fallen headlong, lying belly-down upon the earth. Second, it is nourished by clods of earth, consuming only that which is base and terrestrial. Third - and most telling - it carries its poison in its mouth, and with that venomous tongue it destroys those it bites.

Nothing of this symbolic portrait is missing from the Pleasure-Seeker. He struggles even to lift his head, dragged down and weighed by Excess, which trips and enslaves him. He does not seek the Heavenly Nourishment which Wisdom offers to those who yearn for Divine Sight through Reasoned Principles and Structured-Doctrines. Rather, he pursues the seasonal yields of the earth - what is born of indulgence and harvest - through which come drunkenness, gluttony, and gastronomic bondage. These inflame the Desires of the Belly and awaken the Frenzies Below the Navel.

Such a person labors over rich foods and aromatic dishes, drawn in by the seductive scent of cooking. He circles his mind around the smoke rising from delicacies, and whenever he sees a luxurious table, he collapses upon it, abandoning himself to the feast, striving to ingest everything at once. He does not pursue satisfaction but rather the total consumption of all that has been set before him.

This, too, is why the Serpent is said to bear its poison in the teeth - for the teeth are the agents and ministers of Greedy Desire. They divide and break down whatever can be devoured, delivering it first to the tongue, which evaluates flavor, then to the throat, which swallows without measure. But such excess in consumption is by its nature destructive and venomous, because what is forced inward cannot be fully received: one thing arrives before the last is even digested.

As for the claim that the Serpent speaks with Human Voice, this signifies that Pleasure employs countless champions, heralds, and advance-guard - those who have pledged themselves to her protection and cult, and who shamelessly preach that Pleasure alone rules over all, both great and small, sparing none from her dominion.

LVII. Unions of Male and Female (Pleasure)

Now, the very first unions of Male and Female are inseparably tied to Pleasure as their guiding force. For both sowing and Generation come into being through this Power, and every being that is born is by nature drawn first and most powerfully to her - rejoicing in Pleasure, recoiling from her opposite, Pain.

This is why, even at birth, the newborn cries out, struck by the sudden distress of sensation. For the child, long dwelling in the warm and fiery realm of the womb, is thrust forth all at once into cold air, into an unfamiliar and alien space, and is jarred into suffering. Its cry becomes the clearest signal of its initiation into Pain - the inescapable counter-force to Pleasure.

And so it is said that every living being hastens toward Pleasure as the most necessary and unifying End, and none more so than the Human. The lower animals seek it primarily through taste and reproduction, but Human Beings, possessing Expanded Apprehension, pursue it through all the Senses - chasing after visual splendors, harmonies of sound, and all forms of Delight that may arise through Seeing and Hearing.

Indeed, the accounts are many and varied which celebrate this Experience - Pleasure - as the most native-born, the most kinlike, the most deeply rooted among the Living Beings.

Part VIII: Moses Beyond Plato: Internal-Judgment and the War within the Human Soul

LVIII. The Serpent and Human Speech

Let what has now been said suffice as a paradigmatic sign, explaining why the Serpent was imagined to utter Human Speech. It is for this reason, I believe, that in the particularized Laws - specifically those concerning Beasts, where it is laid out which animals are to be embraced and which to be avoided - there is special attention paid to a creature called the Serpent-Fighter (ophiomachēs, Leviticus 11:22).

This creature, though classed among the Creeping-Things, possesses legs raised above its body, by which it leaps from the ground and springs into the air, much like the kind of locusts or grasshoppers.

But to me, the Serpent-Fighter is nothing else than a symbolic embodiment of Self-Control - a force that wages an unrelenting war and an irreconcilable battle against Lack-of-Control and Pleasure.

For Self-Control cherishes simplicity, restraint, and what is necessary, binding itself to a life of modest dignity and measured sufficiency. Pleasure, on the other hand, revels in luxury, indulgence, and all those excesses of softness and decadence which render both Soul and Body degenerate.

Through these, it comes to pass that Life, for those with Right-Minded Understanding, becomes not only the cause of Death, but a burden more grievous than death itself.

LIX. Woman-Aspect of the Soul

Pleasure, with her sorceries and deceits, does not dare approach the Man-Aspect of the Soul directly - but turns, quite fittingly and with cunning precision, toward the Woman-Aspect and, through her, ensnares the Man as well. For within us, the Mind (nous) holds the place of Man, and the Senses the place of Woman. Now, Pleasure first entangles herself with the Senses, associating and conversing with them familiarly - and through them, she deceives the Ruling-Mind.

Whenever each of the Sense-Apprehensions is captivated by Pleasure's charms, rejoicing in the delights she sets before them, they serve as Handmaidens who present these gifts to their Mistress, the Mind.

So:

For the Eye, Pleasure deploys the serpentine spell of color and form,

To the Ear, she offers melodious harmony,

To Taste, the sweetness of savors,

And to Smell, the fragrance of rising vapors.

These Handmaid-Senses, having welcomed such gifts, bring them forward with gentle persuasion, urging the Mind not to reject anything whatsoever.

And so, the Mind - once lured and seduced - becomes a servant in place of sovereign, a slave in place of ruler, an exile in place of citizen, and mortal instead of immortal.

We must never forget this: Pleasure, like a courtesan and a seductress, yearns to capture a lover. She seeks out procuresses, the Senses, through whom she might hook and bind the Mind. And these Senses, having been ensnared by her enticements, swiftly lead the Mind astray.

They smuggle in the forms of external things, announce them inwardly, and display them as though putting on a show - stamping their Impressions deep into the Mind like seals into wax, and reproducing within the Soul the very same Passion that the external thing excites.

For the Mind, like soft wax, receives the images formed through the Sense-Apprehensions - but, as already said, cannot Grasp the Bodies themselves directly, except by way of these mediating pathways.

LX. First-Humans and Wages of Pleasure

The first humans - those who became slaves to that grievous and hard-to-heal Passion - soon discovered the wages of Pleasure.

For the Woman, the divine account declares, the penalty was piercing anguish: the torments of childbirth, followed by a lifetime of sorrows layered upon sorrows - especially those bound to her children as they are born, raised, fall ill, recover, flourish, or perish. Added to this was the stripping away of freedom, and her subjection to the Dominion of the Man with whom she cohabits - a sovereignty not freely chosen, but one she is compelled to obey under command.

The Man, in his turn, received his share: toils, wearisome labors, and unceasing sweat, all in service of acquiring the basic necessities of life. He experienced a loss of natural abundance - the spontaneous gifts once yielded by the Earth without the aid of agricultural skill - now replaced by a ceaseless struggle, a labor of cultivation required simply to stave off starvation.

One might imagine that just as the Sun and Moon were once for all commanded to shine at the dawn of the cosmos and continue unwaveringly to fulfill that divine charge - driven not by some external necessity but because Wickedness has been banished far beyond the bounds of Heaven - so too the deep and fertile Earth, once untainted, could have borne plentiful harvests in their due seasons without the intervention of farming art or the efforts of cultivating men.

But now the eternal fountains of Divine-Grace have been withheld, since the moment Wickedness began to outpace the Virtues. And so, Grace was no longer granted to the unworthy.

Had the human race been forced to pay the full just penalty for its ingratitude toward its Benefactor and Savior, the Divine, it would have been annihilated entirely. But God, by His nature Merciful, felt Pity and moderated the punishment. He allowed the human race to persist, but no longer did He provide sustenance from the ready bounty of the world. Instead, He made it so that food would not come freely or without effort - lest, afflicted by two evils, both idleness and gluttony, humanity fall into further transgression and outrage.

LXI. Moses' Five Teachings and the Jewish-God

Such, then, was the life of those first humans - who at the beginning lived in innocence and simplicity, but later chose Wickedness in place of Virtue.

Yet through the narrative of the Formation of the Cosmos, the Structured-Revelation offers us many insights. Among them, five rise above all others in beauty and excellence:

First, it teaches that the Divine exists - in refutation of the atheists: those who, wavering in doubt, suspended judgment about the existence of God, and those bolder ones who arrogantly claimed that the Jewish-God does not exist at all - that He is merely a projection of human myths, casting shadows to obscure the Truth.

Second, it proclaims that the Jewish-God is One - countering the advocates of polytheism, who do not blush to transplant the basest regime of mob-rule from the earth up into the heavens, filling the cosmos with a cacophony of lesser gods.

Third, as was already stated, the account declares that the Cosmos is Generated - contrary to those who presume it to be Un-Generated and Eternal, thereby leaving nothing of significance to the Divine.

Fourth, it affirms that the Cosmos is One - since the Eternal-Maker, being Himself One, shaped His Work in likeness to Himself, unifying it according to the principle of Singularity. He used the whole of the material substrate, forming the Whole from all parts - since it could not be Whole unless it arose from the totality of its parts. Yet there are those who claim that many worlds exist - or even infinitely many - but they, being infinitely ignorant, know nothing of Truth. For such matters, one must have right Apprehension.

Fifth, the account teaches that the Jewish-God provides Providence over the Cosmos - since it is necessary that the Maker care for what He has made, just as parents are naturally bound to care for their children, by the Laws and Ordinances of Nature.

Whoever receives these truths - not merely by hearsay, but with Insight, and seals them within his own Life-Principle as wondrous and unshakable forms, that:

1. The Jewish-God exists and truly Is,
2. The Jewish-God is One,
3. The Jewish-God made the Cosmos,
4. The Jewish-God made it One, conforming it to His own singular Unity,
5. The Jewish-God continuously exercises Providence over His Creation -

such a person will live a blessed and flourishing life, marked by doctrines of Reverence and Sanctity, inscribed on the soul like divine impressions.

www.ingramcontent.com/pod-product-compliance
Lightning Source LLC
Chambersburg PA
CBHW081538040426
42447CB00014B/3418